Dedication

For my wonderful daughters Kerry and Adele,
and my darling wife Kathleen.

You have all my love and gratitude.

Acknowledgements

Thank you to all who have made this book possible. To everyone that appears in this book, thank you for your stories, friendship and advice. Most of all, thank you to my family. To Kerry, who made this book happen by simply asking me to write down some of my memories. To Adele, who always encouraged me to keep going. And to my wife Kathleen, who listened and put up with me reading the book out loud night after night as I worked on it.

Finally, a special thanks to the team at Daisa & Co Publishing for all their patience, help and advice in putting this book together.

I hope you all enjoy my book.

Mervin.

MERVIN
DOVE
*— *Tales of a Barton Lad* —*

VOLUME 1

DAISA & CO
• EST. 2003 •

First published in Great Britain in 2017 by:
DAISA & CO
Westfield Lakes, Far Ings Road, Barton upon Humber
North Lincolnshire, DN18 5RG, England

Written by Mervin Dove
Copyright © Mervin Dove 2017
Text copyright © Mervin Dove 2017. All rights reserved.
All material used for this book is from the Author's memory
and personal history. This book is a work of non-fiction based on the true life,
recollections and experiences of the author, seen through the eyes of a young man. In
hoping to make the book more authentic, the author has named everyone truthfully.
The author wishes to express his apologies for any unintentional embarrassment or
offence caused and wishes to express his deepest respect for all mentioned.

ISBN 978 1 9997894 3 5

A CIP catalogue record for this book is available from the British Library.

Book typeset by:
DAISA & CO
www.daisa-co.com

Printed in England

This book is made from paper certified by the Forestry Stewardship Council (FSC).
An organisation dedicated to promoting responsible management of forest resources.

Contents

Introduction

I was born on the 21st November 1941, in Scunthorpe Maternity Wing weighing 11lb 3oz. My Mother was Freda Lucy Dove. My Father was George Burnham Dove.

The first five years of my life were spent at Sedgeworth Farm, Carr Lane, Winterton, where my Grandfather Jesse Taylor was the Foreman for a farming family called Rowsons, in Barton upon Humber.

My sister Pearl was born 20th May 1939. We were both raised with Gran and Pop who were Mam's parents. They were wonderful people, and we will be forever in their debt.

Our Mam died 23rd Sept 1943, which was the reason we were raised with our Grandparents. She was only twenty-two years old, bless her. It is such a shame I don't remember her.

My uncle Ralph was telling me only the other day how he learned of her death. He was working at the time at Vale Farm, Barton, when his boss, Frank Rowson told him he had received a message by telegram and that he had to return home as soon as possible, as Freda had taken a turn for the worse. Ralph explained to me that he had to get cleaned up first, before making the bike ride from Barton to Winterton, to his home. When he arrived, no one was in, so he thought he had better make the bike ride to the Hospital at Scunthorpe.

At that point, a car drove up, and out got Pop.

He said, "It's no good mate, we've lost her." His eyes were full of tears. Poor Gran Taylor was still in the car in pieces, uncontrollable.

That afternoon, Ralph did the milking for Pop. He told me that little Pearl who was four years old then, was opening cupboard doors and looking for her Mam. I was just a baby at twenty months.

He said it was the saddest day ever. With it being September, the main flowers at the funeral were Chrysanthemums. To this day no family member likes the smell of them, but I don't mind them myself.

The funeral came, and Gran Taylor couldn't make it bless her. I try to imagine what it would have been like in the house, absolutely awful beyond words. Little stories about my Mam have been told to me by close family. She loved a good laugh and enjoyed playing the piano and singing. Her final school days were at Grasby.

The family lived at Searby two miles away from the school, so Mam had to walk there and back five days a week. The nearest way was across the fields with her best friend Kathy. Kathy's married name was Petch and she lived in the same home as Ralph and Marjorie. Sadly, she has recently passed away.

Only a few months ago I gave her a photo of Mam and when she held it she kissed it and a tear came. She said, "Poor Freda, she was so lovely and I remember her well." She told me how they would go to Grasby village dances on a Saturday night and have fun and how Mam would always make her laugh. She loved the big band music of the day and a guy called Al Bowlly singing "The Very Thought of You." She left at the age of fourteen and started work as a 'skivvy' at Mill Farm, Top Road, Grasby. This would have been 1934. And she had many stories while working there.

I was told once that the boss' wife decided to have chicken for dinner. Her and Mam caught a chicken in the yard. My Mam chopped its head off while the boss' wife held it down. It then ran around the yard and dropped down dead! This sounds so grotesque now but it certainly would have given them something to chat about over dinner.

Most of the information about Mam has been given to me by Ralph, but Gran was always talking about her and I wished now I had written it all down.

I do remember Gran telling me when they lived at Ferriby Road Corner Barton, Mam used to go down to the Red Lion pub in Junction Square on Friday nights and play the piano and have a good old sing song. She also worked at Hopper's Cycle Works for a while.

Soon after Mam's death, so I have been told, Dad went off to Leeds where he met a lady called Florence. So, we were in the care of our beloved Pop and Gran.

I learned later that Dad came back for us, but Pop told him quite bluntly, that we weren't going anywhere, and told him to leave. That wouldn't happen today I think, but our Pop was a large man and he had served in the First World War out in French trenches fighting the Germans. He was a sergeant in the Lincolns and boxing champ in his group, so it was always a good idea to do as you were told.

Of course, I rarely did that. But I always started off with good intentions. As you will see...

A Pram of Manure

One of the first things I remember is Gran giving me a banana. She had it behind her back as she came up the steps out of the old pantry, and said, "What have I got for you?" Remember these were War years when fruit of that style was hard to come by. How good was that banana? To this day I still love bananas. I take them for my pack up or chopped up in a dish with a sprinkle of sugar and carnation milk.

In the War days, there was a thing called, the 'Black Market.' Gran would make butter, milk curd, and collect eggs from our chickens. All this produce would be sold on to a chap called Ernie Burton, of course keeping some back for our own use. Ernie would come at night after tea on his bike to collect it, and paid Gran cash. It would then end up sold on the 'Black Market.' I remember sitting on his knee whilst he would draw me a traction engine, and how good the drawings were. When people had it hard in the towns, their cities being bombed and not having much food, we had more than enough, and it was all homemade.

There was always a candle in our bedroom so that we could see in the dark. When I was laid in bed I could squint my eyes and the light would be thin lines.

Our toilet was across the yard, (no flush in them days). We had Izal paper that skidded up your bum that fast, it didn't do the cleaning job very well at all!

The first Christmas I remember was when I was about four years old. I got a three-wheel trike. I don't think it was new, but I loved it. I would go up and down the lane, without being bothered by traffic, just folk on cycles now and then.

The year 1947 brought the severe Winter. Heavy snow started in January, and everywhere was cut off.

My uncle Ben was youngest brother to Mam. He was born on the 16th July 1930 and at the time of Mam's death would have been thirteen years old.

He and his friend Colin Walker, from the next farm, had a donkey each, (these were taken in for the Winter from Cleethorpes). Ben made a snow plough out of wood, and him and Col ploughed the road open with donkeys pulling it. That I remember very well.

I distinctly remember wearing long leggings, and walking in the nettles near the back door. But they never stung me.

Something I really enjoyed, was watching the farm workers clean out manure in the crew yard and load it onto tractors and trailers.

I wanted to help, so I got Pearl's pram, and filled it with manure, and toddled off down the lane, about three quarters of a mile over a small wooden bridge which was just wide enough for me and the pram.

Gran realised I was missing, and got on her bike. She found me having a glass of milk at the old lady's house over the bridge, pram parked outside the back door, full of manure.

Poor Gran told me this story when I was much older and still with worry and concern in her voice. I can understand now how she must have felt, especially just having lost our mother. It must have been awful not knowing where I was, especially at that time.

There would always be about six or seven German Prisoners of War living in a large mobile hut outside our farm on the road side. The prisoners worked on the farm, but I'm not sure who provided them with food. I do remember one of them making me a tractor out of wood, (wish I still had it). He had painted it, and I got fresh paint on my fingers.

I remember once Ralph took me to Wintringham railway station on a Bedford Lorry when I was four, with a load of savoy cabbages. Gran used to boil these in the bacon water. The meal was boiled bacon, mashed spuds, and cabbage. I only had the spuds and cabbage, but it was very good.

For cereal, she would steep wash wheat in boiled water until swollen, and then add milk, sugar, and other ingredients. It was so good. It was named, 'Fromaty,' and we had it for breakfast.

Gran would chill our Oatmeal drinks in the cool dairy where she used to churn the butter. Pearl and I used to take it to Pop when he was working in the harvest field, stooking the corn sheaves.

Pop had a pony called Pat and a trap. Back then the corn was cut with a binder, which produced sheaves of corn. These had to be stooked for them to ripen and dry ready for gathering, then taken back to the stack yard by horse and cart and later by tractor and trailer.

In the Winter months, the thrashing contractor would be hired to thrash the corn. It took eight men to do this. Today, a combined harvester can do eighty acres of corn a day with just two men. Back in my farming days it was common to see six or seven men working on a three-hundred-and-fifty-acre arable farm. How times have changed.

So, Pearl and I set off to give Pop his drink. On our way down to the fields, we had a swallow of the drink each and by the time we got there, there was only half a bottle left! Poor old Pop just laughed at us.

Gran used to talk about Clixby Top farm quite a lot when we were all at home, she would say it was the best place they ever lived in, in the days it ranked number one and was owned by Hilton's and Ralph tells me it still is.

In the Spring of that year, Gran, and Pop moved to Barrow Mere, whilst Pearl and I went to live with Ralph and Marjorie at Barton.

The reason for that was that the house attached to the small holding at Barrow Mere was in a poor state. A local rouge had lived in it called Wootten Robbie. He had a bit of a reputation and kept animals he had pinched from the farmers in the area in the house into which we all were moving. How does that sound? He had been evicted, and the property had been purchased by a farmer called Jack. W. Leaning, who also had a large farm about one mile away, down the lane.

This is where Pop would work for the next seven years, walking to work every day with one leg, the other being artificial, because of the First World war. He was capable of doing many duties on the farm, like stacking corn sheaves, making hay stacks, feeding cattle. He wouldn't let his one leg hold him back. Once at thrashing time, where a contractor would arrive with a thrashing drum (combine harvester today) elevator, and Fordson tractor towing it in, a rat ran out of the corn stack, and straight up Pop's artificial leg! One of the men shouted, "Watch out Jesse, that bloody rat has just run up your trouser leg!"

Pop in his stride grabbed it and squeezed it dead, pulled it out, and slung it away. Laughing he said, "That won't run much more!" Pop had seen quite a few rats in the 1914-18 war trenches in France and that one wasn't going to spoil his day.

My Pop was also a master at hedging; this was a well-known trade in the farming world back then. Jack Leaning, the boss and farm owner always said to many folks in and around Barton, that Pop was one of the best hedgers he had ever seen.

Pop was a good gardener, and we used to grow all our own vegetables. The fertilizer came from our

outside toilet, which sounds a bit gross, but the
vegetables were always there in abundance, and tasted
so fresh, and good.

I remember Gran's favourite flower in the summer, it
was called Night Scented Stock, it came in a packet,
and she would sow the seeds just across the yard on
the edge of the lawn. When they grew into their glory,
in the Summer evening, the beautiful fragrance filled
the air. Gran always commented on the smell, and
would say, "Oh don't the Stock smell lovely tonight!"
Back in those laidback days, I remember the Summers
were warm, and lasted for ever.

So, Pearl and I stayed with Ralph and Marjorie at
Barton, while the house was cleaned and decorated.

Just after the war, the colours were very few. I only
remember green, cream, and brown. And in wallpaper
there was very little choice. I remember going on the
bus after school one Summer night, and having tea
with Gran and Pop.

Gran used to make wonderful salads, so tasty. Butter
on the bread all added to the taste. She would flavour
the salads with fresh mint, something we don't do now.
Then we caught the bus back to Barton at the old lane
end and I remember well that Summer night whilst
waiting for the bus, the smell of the hayfield close by,
and sound of the old bus stopping for us.

I think we stayed with Ralph and Marjorie until the
July of that year. She would have been nineteen then.
They lived in a little cottage in Junction Square which
was their first home. Ralph was working then as a

tractor driver for the same farm as Pop, but left soon after and worked for the Barton Council.

Ralph entered a ploughing match at Barton Vale Farm which he won. The tractor was a Standard Fordson with a Ransom semi digger plough for two furrows. The year was 1945 and the prize was £3 which was a lot of money in those days. Pop used to always say that Ralph was a very good tractor driver and could do anything on the farm.

Marjorie and Ralph have always been there for us, like a special big brother and sister-in-law, and at the same time a special aunty and uncle. The little cottage they had was cosy, and we enjoyed being there with them. It must have been a huge commitment for two young people to take on looking after two children. Back then being small, responsibility is something you don't think about though.

Marjorie would make caramel puddings, and I remember her homemade chips were the best. Of course, she could cook anything, and make it good.

Marjorie started me at school in January 1947. I walked with the others and she held my hand and I remember her saying everything would be alright, reassuring me with her soft voice.

I remember my first teacher was a kind lady called Mrs Marrows. Other teachers I liked were Mrs Coulham, and Mrs Snow. I loved being in Mrs Coulham's class as she was a mother figure to me with her kind understanding way. She was always ready to smile and praise you. She also had a daughter called

11

Dawn who we see occasionally and like her mother she is a lovely lady with the same smile. The smell of the class room and school milk I remember well. I didn't like the milk, it was sometimes warm and tasted awful. But some kids from the larger families had two.

I also remember how scary it was, all the kids, and noise at playtime. I was quite timid and shy, and always stood near the wall with another boy called John Shepard. He had a polio leg with a calliper and built up shoe, and we remained good friends all the way through school. I remember seeing a lot of kids with callipers on their legs, but this was quite common back then.

In the canteen, we would queue up at the food hatch and the ladies would serve us. I remember a lady called Mrs Bennett serving us with mashed potato. She was always so nice to me and always cheered me up.

The headmistress of the infants was Miss Lawson, she was quite scary to look at and quite Victorian.

I remember her smacking a boy's backside for throwing conkers in the playground. (Wouldn't happen today). Getting a slap was commonplace, we didn't even say anything when we went home. But I got used to school, and the teachers, and went through the infant classes okay.

Having moved in with Gran and Pop at Barrow Mere, we settled in to catching the service bus every morning at 8.25am. Then there was the long walk from the Market Place all the way to County School across Barton. (Not much time to spare).

Barrow Mere

Waking up in the Winter at Barrow Mere was very cold. Ice on the inside of the bedroom window was common. Pearl and I would scratch our names in the ice, and draw pictures. Gran would get up with Pop at 6am. and light the fire after chopping kindling. So, when we came down, we would sit around the fire. Gran would tell me off for gazing into the fire, day dreaming, and not getting dressed. She would say, "Hey Merv, if you don't hurry you will miss the bus!" Yes, that was me, not Pearl though, just day dreaming me.

In Winter, we would wear a liberty bodice. This was a garment we wore to keep us warm. We wore it next to our skin, it had loads of buttons and if you missed the first one, by the time you got buttoned up, you were lopsided and had to start again.

Breakfast would be Farex. This was made with milk like semolina pudding. Then our toast was done in front of the fire with butter and treacle on.

On entry to the back door (the only door we had) you entered a tin roofed lean-to. When it rained heavy the noise was deafening. My Gran cooked on a primus stove which was on a little table. The lean-to led to our living room which boasted a large coal fired cooking range and side boiler for our hot water. Gran would cook wonderful roasts, cakes, pies, puffed pastry mince pies and much more. The 'posh room' as we called it was next, and we went through that one every night to bed. We only seemed to use that at Christmas but that's how it was in those days with most people. Then upstairs Gran and Pop were on the left, Ben and I were in the front bed room that overlooked the lane and field. Pearl had the back room that overlooked the old yard and paddock. Both rooms were one with wooden boards dividing it to make two rooms.

Whatever the weather, we would walk down the lane to catch the bus to Barton for school. After one year of going to school on the service bus, we got places on the school bus which was much better as we were taken directly to school. The memory of this experience is still quite strong, because when we got on the coach the kids would say "Here are the pigeons coo coo," because our last names were Dove. The name calling soon stopped as we got to know all the kids and made friends with them. Of course, there were always one or two that would have a go, but those few really haven't done much with their lives.

Days at Barrow Mere were lovely. Summer holidays were spent at Beech Grove Farm which was run by Gran's sister, Aunty Kate. She was a widow as her husband, our uncle Norman, had dropped down dead in the barn one year before we arrived at Barrow Mere.

Uncle Arthur was Gran's brother. He was the Foreman, and they lived in the cottage on the farm. Aunty Kate at one side, (best side of course) and Uncle Art, as we called him, with Aunty Phyllis. They had two kids, Jeffrey and David.

Gran and Pop bought me a little red bike from a cycle shop and garage named Grasby's in Barton. I loved it. As I've got older, I wonder how they managed to afford it.

This was to be my transport for the next few years. I would speed up to the farm on summer nights, and play with Jeff at Cowboys & Robin Hood, Roy Rogers, Gene Autry and my favourite, The Durango Kid. He never got killed but the baddies did. We never saw blood. He could take any number of bullets they fired at him and not one went even through his hat! Yes, he was my hero.

One late summer night just after tea, I found I had a puncture in one of my wheels. Gran repaired it for me, and whilst we made sure the puncture held up, we both went brambling across the paddock. We were surrounded with loads of bramble bushes, so it didn't take long to get some.

In the early days at Barrow Mere, our water supply was a large mobile barrel on two wheels, as big as a cart. This was filled at the farm where Pop worked, and brought to our place by a horse named Jack, a big black lovely old thing.

So, can you imagine what wash day was like for my Gran? She would rise at six, light the fire in the kitchen for us, then carry the water from the large water barrel parked at the top of the yard, probably fifteen yards away from the wash house where the boiler was. This would take her twenty minutes, and then she would light the copper fire so she could boil the clothes. The mangle or ringer was in the wash house, this had a stone floor, and she would wear wellies all day, doing it all herself, turning the mangle, hanging washing on the lines to dry. Compare that little story with today's washdays - bung them in the washer, flick a switch, and sit down in a warm house with central heating. Then you put them in a tumble dryer. Ironing is made easy with electric irons and proper ironing boards. Back then ironing was done with old solid irons, which were heated on the open fire grate to the correct temperature for doing the job. Gran would have a thick cloth on the table as an ironing board, and the end result was immaculate. Gran had spent her early teen years in service of the big old houses of the gentry, cooking, washing, cleaning etc. So, our Gran was well equipped to look after our household.

Gran would also boil potatoes in the same boiler she did her washing, (not at the same time of course). These smelled lovely in Winter while they were cooking, Pearl and I would have one with a bit of butter, (very tasty).

Pop would buy two pigs every year which were fed from our scraps. The boiled potatoes were mixed with pig meal, and fed to the pig. We always gave the pigs names, and they would grow into large thirty-two stone animals. So, when it was time for them to be slaughtered, Gran and Pop would say, "George Clayton is coming in the morning. We're going to kill Maisie, or Gertie, or whatever name we had given it. Thing was, we never got upset by this. It was our way of life back then.

George was the local butcher from Barrow on Humber, and had a lovely little green Ford van. He was a proper character with a permanent smile on his face, and used to make us laugh.

On pig kill day, the local bobby would have to be present to witness the kill. This was done with a small hand gun by George the butcher. This was a busy day for everyone, our Gran was up at 6am. to fill the boiler in the wash house with water and light it, so boiled water would be ready to scald the hair off the pig. It would be hung up in the barn on a tripod fashion style timber frame. George would then do the necessary cutting up of the animal, into joints, chines, and other well-known cuts of pork. Gran then would have a full day with Ethel Olingsworth from Winterton, a good friend of the family. She was full of fun, and chased me round the table with the pig's tail. The bladder would be pumped up for us, and we would use it as a football! How does that sound today?

When Gran made the large bowls of sausage meat, she would put a taster in the oven, to see if she had got the mix right. It tasted fantastic with her homemade bread and homemade butter spread liberally on. Her pork pies, Haselet and pig fries were excellent. The large flicks of ham were hung from the ceiling on meat hooks in the cool part of the kitchen. These were salted with pig salt, a little courser than table salt. This used to be delivered from our grocer in Barton in large blocks. Pearl and I would grate it down to its powder form in a wooden tub, where we would be knelt near the fire with graters. I remember if you had a cut anywhere on your hands, it would really smart. Of course, Pop would say; "It weren't hut ya boy, it's onny a cut!"

Of course, I often got myself into scrapes. I spoke before about Gran's mangle, well I once thought I would try and flatten a saucer by putting it through the ringer. Well of course it broke into many bits and cut the rubber rollers. This would be a talking point for a few years to come, and yes, I got a slap! By the time we replaced it with a more modern machine, the rubber rollers had opened, and weren't very good. But this was 1949 and Gran had to wait until we moved to Barton to get her Twin Tub until 1953.

Playing at Beech Grove was fun. We had all the stack yard and the long thin forest, or planting, as my Uncle Art called it. We would make tree houses for dens and go exploring. The forest continued all the way from Beech Grove to Caistor Road.

Many times, in the bramble season Auntie Phyllis and her relations, who were Auntie Annie, her sister, her daughter Christine, Audrey who was Jeff's cousin and Audrey's Dad George would come over from Scunthorpe along with us kids to go into the wood picking brambles and get loads. I've seen her take white enamel buckets and fill them too.

One night Ben made me a trolley. This was fantastic and was to be very successful for a few things. I spent hours with Neville Chapman, Alan Curtis, and Tich Paul, using my trolley to go fishing and to roam the old clay pits area.

The boy's parents were lovely people. Mrs Paul, Tich's mum, always made a bit of a fuss with me and was very caring.

Today, mainly in the Assembly Rooms at Christmas, we enjoy listening to Tich sing whilst his cousin Nev plays the base guitar in a group, Nev has always played in various bands in his life, whilst Tich is famed for singing with a well- known band The Echoes; who supported Frank Highfield, Mike Sarne, and Bert Weedon and although our lives have taken different directions and drifted apart, it's so special to know all these years on we are still good friends.

Jeff and I would get a load of logs from Auntie Kate's log pile, and go all the way round the stack yard hiding until we got to the lane on the way to our house. You see our Auntie Kate never thought to say, "Merv, take your Grandma some logs. Or just help yourself." So, you could say, Auntie Kate forced us to steal.

On arrival at Grans, she would say, "Well done lads," and give us a cake or something good like that.

Then we would go back and steal another load, filling her coal house up for the winter. I am so pleased we did that for her, not realising how it helped her with the coal bill until later in life, when she would reminisce, smile, and tell the story about her sister's logs which ended up on her fire via my trolley.

My old friend Geoff and I won the Soap Box Derby with the trolley at the Barton Carnival one warm Saturday afternoon. Our reward was 5 shillings/or 25p. The weekly wage back in 1951 was about £2.75p. Can you imagine how much Vimto and Smiths that would buy? Smiths later became Walkers and was based in Lincoln. The crisps were lovely, and had the little blue bag of salt in so you sprinkled it yourself, no multi flavours then.

In the Summer months at Barrow Mere, at the bottom of the lane, the Gypsies would camp with their old horse drawn caravans. They would always come up the lane with their large water cans, and ask us for water. In exchange, they would give Gran some clothes pegs they had made from carved ash and thin strips of tin cut from tin cans. This was wrapped around the top of two shaped sticks and then nailed with a small tack nail.

I remember, we used to have an old bloke called Blacky. He used to arrive on a carrier bike. This was a strong bike which had a large carrier on the front, which held his wares. He would sell Pop a pair of trousers, or a jacket, shirt, socks, you name it. He came from Hull on the ferry, and would travel around our area, Barton, Barrow, New Holland, and other local villages. Well Saturday lunch time, he called and he would call my Pop "Governor." Anyway, Pop had bought a pair of trousers from him a few weeks before, and he didn't like how they fitted. So Blacky arrived and shouted, "Are ya in governor?" We were all sat round the table eating Gran's homemade bread cakes and sausages with lovely rich gravy.

"So Blacky," said Pop.

"Now then governor, how's things today?"

"Not bad," said Pop. "Them bloody trousers you sold me don't fit very well, so I'd better have my money back!"

Gran looked a bit uneasy as she had seen Pop before when he's made a point.

Blacky said, "Nay, nay governor, I can't give you ya money back, ya bought as seen!"

"Well," Pop said, "Shut that door mother."

Gran got up, and shut the door. Ben's looking at Pop who by now was standing up, and I thought all hell's going to break loose.

Blacky said, "Well maybe this time governor, I can give ya money back."

"That's a good lad Blacky," said Pop sitting down again, "Now don't miss ya ferry back home, and we'll bid ya good day!"

That's how it was then. Pop had seen too much in the war days to let somebody like Blacky bother him. We all settled back into our dinner and nothing else was said about it.

Snake Belts & Braces

I remember asking my Gran for a Snake Belt. These were very popular with young lads back then. They were named so because they had a metal shaped snake which was a hook to fasten the belt together. The belt itself was heavy elastic coloured, mine was brown and yellow. Anyway, Gran kept saying no.

"You keep your braces," she said, which were hideous things.

One day, Pop said, "Come and see me in the sugar beet field where I'm working, and I will give you the half-a-crown (25p) for the belt. Pop was chopping out sugar beet at that time. This process was done with a hoe. You had to leave a single plant, and on average, you would do eight acres each paid by piece work. This was £4 to £5 per acre, and it was possible to do two to three acre a week. I still have Pop's hoe.

So, there I am running across the field Saturday lunch time, and Pop with his dry humour, said;

"Nar then boy, wot you after?"

Smiling, I said, "Money for my belt please."

"Aw well, ya better av this then."

He gave me half-a-crown with a big grin. So off I went on my bike to Barton. I would be about nine or ten at this time. Going on the main road wasn't a problem back then, I might have seen four or five cars all the way there and back.

My destination was Kenny Milson. He had a gentleman's clothes shop in George Street, next to the George Hotel. In the Summer months, and good weather through the Winter, he would hang wellingtons, work boots (hob nail with a steel toe cap), donkey jackets (thick ¾ length coats with leather shoulders) and other work attire outside his shop. He also made ice lollies. You could either have a weak one, or very strong one. No normal ones as he never got the mixture just right. So, in the shop I went, leaving my bike outside propped on the footpath quite safely, without fear it would be stolen in those days.

Kenny, grinning away, with his trilby hat on, suit complete with waistcoat, and brightly coloured cravat, said, "Hello Mr. Taylor," with a stammer, "How are you today?" Excited, I said, "Could I have that brown and yellow snake belt please?

"Of course," says he, going to great lengths to let me know that; "These are all in now."

He also had an old guy with him all the time, called Gilbert. He too would put his sales talk to good use, backing up every word Kenny said and they also sniffed snuff which would be sprinkled on their jacket lapels and Ken's moustache. It was always an experience visiting Kenny Milson's shop.

I had the belt for a few years, and Gran would remind me not to keep hitching my trousers up, or she would take it off me and put me back to braces (of course, she never did).

One of my chores on getting home from school was to fetch the milk in a milk can that hung on my handle bars. No matter what the weather, I had to do it. The dairy was on the farm about a mile away, where my Pop worked. A lady called Violet was the chief dairy hand, she had a weathered complexion, and was only five feet tall. I remember her wellingtons. She wore them much bigger than they needed to be. They used to joke about Violet.

"I hear Violet's gone to the docs complaining of red thighs. Doc says she needs six inches cutting off the tops of her wellies!"

But she had a heart of gold, and would do anything for anybody. She worked at Leanings for more than fifty years biking from Barton every day in all weathers. Her hours were 5.30 in the morning until late.

I sometimes had to wait for the milk because I would get there whilst the cows were being milked. The milk would pass through the separators to get the quality milk. So, I would sit on cow cake bags and wait, keeping a close eye on the milking staff, watching they didn't squirt me with milk as they sometimes did.

In the Summer nights, I would have my tea, then straight up to Beech Grove to play with Jeff. Sometimes, Auntie Phyllis (Jeff's Mam) would boil some new potatoes, dug straight out of the garden, with a sprig of mint in the water, let them cool and slice them, and fry them up until golden brown in a large frying pan. She would serve these up with bread and homemade butter. They were so good, what a memory. We all loved Auntie Phyllis for her sweet ways, and cooking. She used to tell Jeff and I to come to her sliding pantry window, where we would find her homemade jam tarts and other lovely pastries! They were regular throughout our childhood.

One weekend, I stayed for a sleepover, and when we went to bed, she leaned over to kiss Jeff goodnight, and gave me a kiss too. That was special. But our Gran always kissed us good night too.

I remember the first time Jeff and I got air rifles. Mine was a 'Diana' air pellet gun. They were quite weak, but at close range, you could kill a Sparrow! One summer night, I shot a Swallow by mistake, and to this day it still makes me feel sad that I did it. After that, guns didn't interest me, and when I see a Swallow now, I am reminded of that awful night.

The memories at Barrow Mere are endless. We would climb trees, play conkers down at Barrow Park, where there were loads of lovely big conker trees. At the main entrance to the park from Barrow, stood a large orphanage, run by some people call Fenner, they were nice folk. They had a golden Labrador dog, and it always found its way to our house, and sometimes wouldn't go home. Pearl always made a big fuss of it.

Its name was Blondy, and it got on very well with our dog Lady, who was a collie.

One summer night, Pearl took Blondy home, and explained to the Fenners that Blondy was a regular visitor to our house. They smiled and said they hardly ever saw her, that she seemed to be happy with Pearl, and so my sister could have her. Pearl was so excited when she came back with her and Blondy stayed with us for quite a few years until she started having fits, and we had to have her put to sleep.

Barrow Park held events like pageants, where the local folk would dress up and sing songs. I remember one year, they had a Maypole. This was a large pole with coloured ribbons hanging down from the top, and girls danced around it holding a ribbon each until it formed a red, white and blue design all the way down the pole. This was done to music played by the local village band.

We also played at home too, in the Summer we would make a house out of old bedding Gran had given us. This would be put up with help of two clothes props tied and held in the low branches of the apple trees in the orchard. We would have our lunch in it. Gran was always on hand to do us sandwiches and homemade cakes, Vimto was our favourite drink to wash it down, or Gran would make oatmeal drink. It was so refreshing.

We also had a tortoiseshell cat called Tiny. She would follow us all over. Regularly, she would meet the bus in at the bottom of the lane along with Lady, the collie, and the pair of them would wait for Gran getting off the bus. They really were intelligent.

I remember one night coming home from playing at Beech Grove, I'm coming down the lane on my trusty little bike, and discovered I had no brakes! Gran fortunately was outside doing something near the gate. I'm shouting, "Gran! Gran! I can't stop!" She says, "Aim at me, and I will stop you."

Well, we both ended up in the grass in a heap. Poor old Gran, but neither of us were hurt.

In the last few days of the Summer holidays, Gran would take me down to Barton, to a gentlemen's and boy's outfitters called Fred Canty. His shop was in Fleetgate, next to what is now Fred Clipson's Barton Museum. She would buy me a new dark green corduroy wind cheater, with grey flannel trousers. Then to Stead & Simpson's in the market place for new shoes. This must have been expensive, even back then, because Pearl had the same spent on her too. We were so lucky, even some kids at school who had parents weren't dressed as well as us.

I remember seeing a pair of wellington boots with a Dunlop badge on the front in orange. They were a proper dull grey colour like adult ones and not shiny black kid's material. Gran bought these for us too and I loved them. This would be our winter clothing. It kept us lovely and warm whilst waiting for the school bus at the bottom of the lane.

When we were about nine or ten years old, Gran started taking us to Cleethorpes for the day. This would be on the bus, in the summer holidays. The coach driver was called Freddy Clarke, and the bus conductor was Frank Gray. In those days, everybody knew everybody. It was a single decker coach, operated by Lincolnshire Roadcar, painted green, with gold lettering. The coach would take us through all the villages on its way to Cleethorpes, so the journey would take about one hour. On arriving at our destination, we would make for the beach.

Gran would always pack us up for a picnic on the beach and she would buy a jug of tea from one of the many tea stalls that were on the beach back in those days.

On one particular trip to Cleethorpes, our Gran had received some child allowance money. she had fought hard for many years she told us. The amount she had in her purse was about four or five pounds, which was a lot of cash in those days.

She said, "Today we will have a treat, and have fish and chips." Steel's Corner House even back then was a thriving fish restaurant, so that's where we went for our lunch. I only vaguely remember Gran losing her purse that day. I remember Gran saying she had paid for the meal, and put her purse on her knee. When she stood up she forgot her purse was on her knee, and it fell to the floor. We walked out of the restaurant, and after heading back to the beach, she realised. She dashed back, but it had gone. Day ruined, we went home. She never did get over it. It would be a regular topic in the following years, bless her.

We would also visit Auntie Alice, Gran's sister. She lived at Wootton, and was married to John Firth, local wheel wrights, and joiners. She was a lovely lady, very kind. They had a large back garden, with a small fish pond surrounded by small fir trees. I still remember the smell of those trees. She would fuss over us, and give us cold drinks; she was quite close to Gran. So, when the news came she was ill, Gran was over to see her. Unfortunately, her illness was quite serious, and she died shortly of pneumonia after Gran got there. I remember Gran coming home afterwards, and crying. Our Gran had more than her share of sadness in her life.

On winter nights in Barrow Mere with just one fire in the kitchen to warm the whole house, the bedrooms were very cold.

Gran would say, "Would you like a shelf in your bed?" This was a shelf out of the oven, that was wrapped up in a sheet, and placed in the bed. It made it lovely and warm. When Gran came to bed she would take the shelf out while we were asleep. (Recalling all these memories, my Gran should be called an angel).

I remember in the winter nights we would listen to the radio which was a treasured piece of equipment. The make of this radio was a Cosser and it operated on a large battery 8" x 10" in size, also an accumulator. This was a liquid battery which was charged up by the local radio shop in Barton, called Parks. Mr Parks would arrive once a month in his little van, and change it for us. The reception was hit and miss, but once tuned in, it was quite good. Every night, we would gather round the radio, with a good fire going, and listen to The Archers, An Everyday Story of Country Folk, as they used to advertise it. Then Friday nights brought us a programme called Up the Pole with Jimmy Jewell, and Ben Warris, they made us laugh, as it was a comedy show. The other programs we loved were; Ted Ray, in Ray's a Laugh, with Kitty Bluett. There would be a musical break with a song by Donald Peers. One of his songs was In a Shady Nook.

On Sunday lunch times, we would have the radio on Forces Request. All the latest songs were played, requested by the lads in the Army, Navy and Air force.

Gran and I would also play cards at the table, the kitchen was lit with an Aladdin Lamp, which ran on pink paraffin, and had a tall clear glass chimney, which gave out the light from a mantle, which was very delicate, like if the back door was opened, the draft would blacken one side of it, Gran would hurry us to shut the door.

One night after listening to my favourite programme Up the Pole, they announced it would finish, never to return. Well, I cried. Gran was there to comfort me and said, "Come on Merv, let's have a game of cards." She was always there for us, (and Pop of course), but I have to say, Gran was more compassionate.

She did everything for us. Even horrible things. Making the journey across the yard at night to the earth closet for a wee wasn't a good experience. We used to have a little Kelly Lamp and had to shield the wind from it to stop it going out. The toilet was in the corner about twenty yards away. If it wasn't windy, we would take a candle. I used to like to singe the cobwebs, and burn the spiders! (Out of fear, I think). Sounds awful now, but at the time, I thought it was ace! For our night pees, we all had a poe under the bed, or bed chamber as they called it. This would be emptied every morning by our poor Gran. She used pine smell disinfectant then, a fresh smell. House work back then was a full-time job. Gran told us she learnt the skills of baking, and all the keeping house techniques during her days in service.

Christmas at Barrow Mere was always exciting for Pearl and me, although our Grandparents hadn't much money, we always had a lovely surprise for a gift. I remember one Christmas, I had been going on about a "Chad Valley" Fordson Major toy tractor, that I wanted for my gift. In Barton, there was a large hardware store in George Street called Dewey's, and they had a wonderful toy department that I used to look around whenever I got the chance. On the build up to Christmas, I saw this Fordson tractor in there, I just used to stand and look at it, (not allowed to touch it) just dream that I might have one somehow. Well this particular Christmas, I woke about 5am, and there at the bottom of the bed was a large brown paper parcel, and to my delight there it was – my tractor. How poor old Gran and Pop managed it, I will never know. I wish I could talk to them about things now and tell them how grateful we were.

Christmas back then was so magical and special with harsh winters, white frost, and snow making it all one lovely scene. Because of money shortages, Gran would make practically everything. All she would buy were basics like, flower, sugar, gravy browning, cereals, dried fruit and Carnation milk that I still buy, and love. Killing two pigs every year would give us lard, all the pork we could eat, pork pies, sausages, sausage rolls, Haslett, brawn and scraps.

Gran would make lovely puffed pastry mince pies, Christmas puddings, and Christmas cake, fully iced. She always made our butter, fresh curd for her lovely milk curd tarts. Other food from the land was Rabbit, Pheasant, Brambles, and Mushrooms. Roast rabbit how Gran did it was so tasty, and roast pheasant was delicious.

One year, Gran said "Let's make some paper chains for Christmas." This was done cutting thin strips of old wall paper, and gluing them together, (homemade glue), then when they were dry we hung them from corner to corner in the front room. We thought they were great. Gran would build a lovely big log fire, and the special smell of it all is still with me today as I recall these wonderful memories. A coal fired house has a special smell, that's warm, and friendly, we also had a lot of love in our house too.

When we had big winter fires, you could hear the back boiler bubbling away, but we always had hot water. Oh yes, we had to fill the boiler by hand of course, carried from the water cart.

Always at Christmas we would have a new Snip Rug in front of the fire, this of course was made from cut up old clothes. Thin strips of clothing about six inches long were folded to make it double, and snipped into a freshly washed Sugar Beet pulp bag, which formed the underside of the rug. The snipper was just a simple wooden handled gadget, with a sharp point, and a sprung loaded finger to hold the piece of cloth, so you pushed it through the sacking, and twisted it pulling through again. But they were lovely and warm on the winter nights. Another carpet that we could afford was Coconut Matting, a very hard-wearing factory woven hessian, with red or green bordering. In the Spring, Gran would take the carpet up. Take it outside, give it a good beating. Where the mat had been on the floor, all the dirt would collect. Of course, Gran didn't have a vacuum cleaner, that came later when we moved into Barton.

One Winter, Ben had a sledge made for Pearl and me. A small family firm in Winterton made it out of half a tube of steel, and delivered to the house one snowy night, we were so excited, and couldn't wait to test it out the following morning. It was to be a great success once Ben had fitted some small planks on the top frame so we could sit on it.

Ben was like a big brother, uncle, and best friend, all the things he did for us were endless. On Friday nights at the tea table, we would be sat down ready to eat,

Pearl, and I would sit opposite Ben, with Pop on my left at the head of the table, and Gran would sit at the other end. Ben, as a surprise for me would place a Dinky Toy on my plate - a tractor, car, lorry, or fire engine, and many, many more. Pearl would get her pocket money instead.

He was friends with the neighbour, Alan Hunt, who had a small holding just up the lane, and some nights they would go down to Barton fish and chip shop in Alan's little car, and he would get Pearl and I a bag of chips each for our supper. The taste of those chips is still with me. So, when it came for Ben to receive his papers for the Forces, we were a bit sad to say the least. It was to be just after his 21st birthday July 1951, which he celebrated on Aunty Kate's lawn. It was a large party, and we all sat round a big table. The weather I remember was glorious. For me it was special, because I wore grey flannels with my snake belt to hold them up (not silly braces!) Ben was emptying the outside toilet. This was dumped on the garden, and dug into, yes, we grew some damn good vegetables. Pop used to say, "You can't beat a bit of shit on ya garden."

Anyway, that summer evening, Gran came out with a large brown envelope for Ben. It said, *"On His Majesties Service."*

Ben said, "What the bloody hell is this?"

Pop says, "It's ya papers boy, ya going in the Forces!"

So, Ben had to leave us for the two-year National Service, as it was known in those days. He went in the Royal Engineers Army, and did very well, achieving Lance Corporal in the Military Police. We couldn't wait for him to come home on leave as he did every few months.

Ben was engaged to a young girl call Win. They were in love, and so happy. So, the day Ben went off into the army, it was doubly sad. Win had auburn hair, was petite, and quite stunning. She was a good friend to us, and made us laugh. They were to stay together for the next year.

Whilst Ben was in the army, Win was working on the Lincoln Castle New Holland to Hull Ferry, serving tea and refreshments in the buffet, and this is where she met her future husband, Tim West. Very sad for us all. But Ben got his 'Dear John' letter, and had to get over it, as we did. It was strange without her company, as she was always with us. But Tim was a good man, and she had a happy marriage, with two kids. Sadly, Tim died after twenty-six years married to Win, but she is still alive at eighty.

Ben would come home on leave, and he played games with us, we never wanted him to go back, but his army days were soon over.

Whilst Ben was in the army, I got friendly with Geoff Nicholson, who was to become a lifelong friend. Geoff would come up to Barrow Mere and we would climb trees, and play on the trolley. He would cycle to our house from his place on Barrow Road at Barton, where he lived with his Mam, Auntie, and cousin Dennis. He would stay for his dinner in the summer holidays. Gran would do us potato scallops, (slices of potato dipped in batter), with bread and butter. When you put a sprinkle of vinegar on them, they used to crackle, and they were delicious.

At the bottom of the lane across the main road, there was a paddock with loads of mushrooms.

One evening Pearl and I went mushrooming there, and found many, but one we found was as big as a dinner plate! We took them all home, and Gran cooked the big one for our supper, and made lovely gravy with it, of course we had homemade bread and butter to mop it up! Then the following morning, we would have what was left over of them for breakfast, they always seemed to taste better second time around. In the orchard, we had a Damson tree, (small, black plums) and a Victoria Plum tree, (large, red plums) lovely, and sweet. Gran would make jam out of these, it was delicious.

I have to tell you about the stuffed Chine she once did. This was a large ham Chine, cut from the pig we had killed. This would be diced with a sharp knife, and then stuffed with a mixture of; parsley, chives, onions, and bread. All this would be put through the hand mixer. Gran would then stuff the mixture in the diced chine. Having done this, she would wrap it up in an old cotton sheet, and boil it in the copper. It would boil slowly for a while until cooked. Gran's timing was always spot on, as it was always nice and tender, it tasted delicious. Her cooking talents were endless.

As I got older, on Harvest Nights, Jeff, my cousin and I would drive the tractor on from corn stook, to corn stook for the men to collect in the harvest, which helped them a lot, because they didn't have to climb on and off the tractor every two minutes. Of course, I had to be in bed for 8.30pm back then, so I would be laid in bed, and about 9.30pm as it was getting dark, the workmen from the farm cycled past our house going home. My bedroom was in the front, (as they all knew) and as they were passing our house, in harmony, they would all shout; "Good night Merv!" I can still hear them as I recall this memory.

Nocca Jackson, first name Norman, he was head tractor driver, Curly Curtis, was the Garth Man, (looking after live stock) and milking cows etc. His nick name came from his 'bald head.' His son Joe swapped me an Ingersoll pocket watch for 10 Players cigarettes. These cost one shilling and sixpence (7½ pence). I still have it and it still works. I had to bike down to Barton with advance pocket money from dear Gran to buy the fags. Yes, back then they sold them to you, no problem. Having bought the fags, I rushed back all excited to get my watch. The other men were Edwin Franklin and Jim Sargant. Jim Sargant, married Aunty Kate's daughter, Faith.

When the harvest was gathered in and all stacked in the stack yard, it was always a lovely site, about ten corn stacks all netted down with straw to look like thatched roofs. Auntie Kate would arrange a harvest supper in the barn to celebrate the safe gathering in of the harvest. The barn would be cleaned out and decorated with cornsheaves, flowers, and decorations. The whole barn was illuminated.

I will always remember the 'Giddy Keepers,' who attended one year, two retired teachers who were sisters. They were quite Victorian in their dress. We had returned home after the supper and Pop was sat in the garden when they passed. He told us after that they were giggling and laughing as they walked down the lane, swearing about how the rich food had given them such gas. Pop often laughed at that because they were usually so prim and proper.

Large hams, Gran's stuffed chine, pork pies, sausage rolls, brawns, large bowls of salad, homemade cakes, mountains of sandwiches, sherry trifles, the food was endless, and of course beer and wine, lemonade etc.

Some of the men would sing and play the squeeze box which was like a small Accordion. Some would tell stories. We played games and generally had a good time.

It was Jim's job to drive Aunty Kate and Faith down to Barton to do their weekly shop every Saturday morning. The car was a Standard 14 and she would go to the bank first, and draw out the men's wages for the week. Then she would go to the various shops; Frank Potts in the market place, general store. (a larger version of Arkrights). Also on hand were Birketts fresh bread, and cakes, Smiths Butchers, Eastows vegetables and fresh fish, and many more, yes all in the Market Place. Aunty Phyllis was a lovely Auntie, who would bike down to Barton on a Saturday afternoon with her shopping bags to do her weekly shop, with bike back loaded up. She would always call at our house on the way back, and have a cup of tea, and a chat to Gran and Pop. Poor old Phyllis had no idea of time and at about 6pm she would look at the clock, or Gran would say, "What's for tea tonight then?" and Auntie Phyllis would say; "Mable, is that the time? I must be getting off, Arthur will be wondering where I am." (This was every Saturday, quite funny really). But there were no car lifts with Aunty Kate for her. We saw her wet, cold, and hot, with her pile of shopping, but she never complained and never got a lift with her sister-in-law.

About 1949 - 50, it was a dark time for Gran. I think it was a nervous breakdown she suffered, however this is where Ralph and Marjorie once again stepped in and Gran, along with Pearl and I moved into their House at 51 Bowmandale, Barton. This was their second home, a new council house. Back then building was going on all the time. Gran was in a bed in the front room, it seemed like forever she was ill, but I loved being there. New friends to play with and street lighting too. Ralph and Marjorie were marvels once again, taking care of things for us. It was so easy going to school living in the town, and walking with the other kid's. After six months, Gran recovered and we moved back to Barrow Mere until 1953 when we moved into Barton permanently.

Growing up in Barton

1953 saw us move into 14 Harrowdyke, Barton. New council houses were being built at great speed trying to get back to normal to re-house families' after the war years. Ours was three bedrooms. I always remember the lovely fresh smell in all the rooms, freshly decorated. Most of all, nobody had lived in it. Poor old Gran was in heaven, we couldn't believe our luck, and it was only a council house. It had one radiator in the dining room, which was heated from the back boiler in the front room. This was to be our first experience of having an inside flush toilet, and a bathroom, along with electric lights with wall sockets and a gas cooker. Hot water came from either the immersion heater, or the coal fired back boiler. It was real luxury, believe me, from Barrow Mere, to all this.

I used to go up to do some shopping errands for Marjorie, at this time two new shops had opened on Bowmandale, Ferribys and also Appleyards. Mr Ferriby had played a small part in getting us the council house we had just moved into to, he was a likable man.

Going to school was a pleasure, a five-minute walk with my mates, and later on my bike. This bike was a hand me down from Ben, but it had gears, and I loved it. School was good days, but I only liked a few lessons - Woodwork, Art, Drawing, and a little English. I was always told, "Mervin could do much better if he paid more attention," but I don't think it's held me back in life.

I have to tell you about the rolling pin I made for Gran. This was done in my woodwork lesson on a wood turning machine, it only had one handled end as I couldn't get the same at the other end, but Gran loved it, don't know what happened to it though. Then we had cookery lessons, and I remember making some Raspberry Cakes once, but got a slap from Miss Credland for tasting the mixture whilst I was preparing it. I remember being in Harry Furniss' class, and every Friday afternoon he would read a few chapters of books, Tom Sawyer, Treasure Island, and many more. He was such a good reader that you felt you were actually in the story.

I remember once when I was in the Juniors, I came first in a handwriting competition, my prize was a pack of Plasticine. That must have encouraged me to do more handwriting! Should it have been a pen instead?

Also, I came first in an Art Competition, can't remember what my reward was for that one. But little did I know how significant this was to be years down the road of my life. Those two competitions would play a major part in my life, in me becoming a Sign

Writer. My art teacher Alf Poole was a wonderfully gifted artist, and encouraged me a lot.

But back then all I had in mind was to be a tractor driver on the farm. So, you could say, I just breezed my way through school, and couldn't wait to leave.

Two years before leaving school I got a Grocer round at a shop down the High Street called Nicholson's. The wage per week was £1.20, the week was every day except Thursday, and Sunday. So, after school, off I would go, and load up my carrier bike. My round was, Queens Street, Queens Avenue, Butts Road, Marsh Lane, Pasture Road, and Beck Hill.

My first day was Friday, I remember it well. Late September, very warm, and the High Street was busy, as it always was on a Friday in those days. I had loaded the large basket with all the customers' provisions purchased earlier that afternoon to be delivered. I went inside the shop for the final delivery details, when I heard an almighty crash. I dashed outside, and to my horror, the bike had fallen over, and spilled all the contents in the high street. There it was, eggs, flower, biscuits, a Lucozade bottle, smashed, sugar, you name it! And on my first day.

Mr Nicholson, my boss, said not to worry. And suggested in the future it might be a good idea to ask Eddie (the other grocer boy) if he could mind the bike for me while I was in the shop. Yes, he was a kindly old man, with whom I got on well. As the months rolled on, I grew to like it more and more.

It was our job to go and collect sugar and other provisions from Lea's in George Street. We would pick up the two stone of bagged sugar parcel, and place it in the carrier on front of the bike. We would have four stone in total, and pedal back to the shop, only to lift it off again, and stack it in the shop. (Yes, at thirteen!)

I purchased my first bike with my earnings from the grocer round, it was a Sun Vitesse, lovely cherry red, white wall tyres, cream seat, and saddle bag to match. It had a Miller lighting system, and three speed sturmey archer gears. I had to raise £3.00 for the deposit. Ralph was my Guarantor. I still got pocket money from Ben, and a bit from Gran, so I could still go to the pictures etc. Also, the people I delivered to seemed to think I was a bit special, because as I got to know them, I would do little tasks for them, like get the coal in, move a bit of snow in the winter, and chop wood for the fire. Because they were mostly elderly, and some were on their own, they just wanted a little chat.

"What have you been up to at school today?"

If the old man was there, he would say. "Have yer got yer eye on them lassies yet mate?" That would be Mr Thompson saying that, and his wife would say; "Now then stop that talk Bert!" Mrs Thompson was lovely, if it was wet weather, she would dry my hair, and I would have a warm drink.

Then there was Mr and Mrs Bland on Butt's Road, wonderful old people. Warm drinks, cakes, sweets, always something for me. At Christmas time, it was common to be given 2s.6p (half a crown) 12.5p, keep in mind, my wages were £1.20 per week. So, I did rather well, but because my round in the week was mainly fresh bread, the advantage was, I saw them three or four times a week.

My bread basket was quite large, and the bread was placed in old biscuit tins wrapped in tissue paper, to hold this in place, Miss Nicholson, the shop keeper would put the customer's name on a piece of paper, then place a meat skewer through and into the bread to hold the paper in place. It was my task to make sure the bread didn't get wet when it rained, no white gloves or hygiene stuff then to complicate the job. Some of the bread was factory wrapped though, but that would be sliced. The company back then who supplied the sliced bread we used were from Grimsby, it was called Glentons and employed a lot of people. So, my grocery boy days were very enjoyable.

At the same time as I was at Nicholson's doing my grocer round, Geoff was working at Potts in the Market Place doing the same. Geoff's round was harder than mine, and I remember his earnings were fifteen shillings a week. He had to deliver animal feed as well as groceries, and all on a carrier bike.

When I was growing up in Barton, I began to notice a few memorable characters. One chap was called George Small, who the local fish and chip shop people would hire to fetch their fish from Barton Railway Station fresh from Grimsby Docks. He had a two-wheel running barrow, which held one case, but he used to get the job done.

Then there was Bill Thew who had a speech problem. This sounds awful now, but us lads would sometimes mock him. I have seen him bike to work with a hurricane lamp on the front of his bike, it lit the whole street up. too. Everybody loved Bill, he did a lot for the Salvation Army. He would go out to the surrounding villages selling War Cry Magazines year after year and when they would play Christmas carols on the green opposite our house in Harrowdyke, Bill would go around the houses with a collection box.

Then there was Kenny Robinson, and Walla Dent. Kenny would follow the lads round who emptied the dustbins and Walla used to go around the town in a bath chair.

You don't see these now, it had two large wheels on the rear, and a small one on the front. It operated like a cycle, but instead of using your feet, it was your hands that propelled you along. Walla could go very fast in his bath chair, also he was a lovely friendly man, always had a smile, and he would remember all our names as we passed by. It would be "Hi Walla," then coming back you would hear, "Hi Merv, Hi Geoff," echoing down the street.

Another character P.C. Arnett, was a Bobby in the town, us lads feared him. If you had a light out, or rode on the footpath, you were for it. The bell had to be working and mudguards on.

All the shop owners seemed to be funny people, always up for a laugh. In those laidback lovely days, with not many cars about, everybody had time for a chat. It was common to see gangs of men on their way back to work gathering outside the railway station on their bikes, just chatting away, and having a laugh.

Back in the early fifties we had Carnivals in the park, and Gymkhanas, with the local farmers bringing in the ponies, and their daughters of course to ride them. Stalls would be around the ring, and down the sides of the lane coming in. Vimto and Smiths Crisps were the main items to buy, along with other goodies to tempt you.

Neil Story, brother of my friend Dave worked at Pinchbeck's electrical shop in George Street and helped to fit all the loud speakers up in the park for the carnival days. As a young lad Neil was very funny and made us all laugh.

The Carnivals were the best for me, because many Barton companies would have a Float which was a decorated lorry, with children dressed up to create all kinds of lovely scenes. The companies back then taking part would be; The Farmers Company, Hoppers Cycle Works, Osgerby's Haulage, some local builders, Brick Yard Workers, The Salvation Army, the Town Brass Band, Iris Vrabel and her dancing girls, and of course, many more. Sadly, most of the named companies are no longer.

Recalling these memories brings back the freshly cut grass smell in the wonderful old park, it was always freshly prepared ready for the big day, and oddly enough, I don't remember many wet ones, the sun always seemed to shine to complete a lovely day.

When the fair visited Barton, it was so exciting, I couldn't wait to get there. I still have memories of the men who used to work on the rides, and can hear the latest music being played on the old vinyl 78's. This could be heard quite a way off if the wind was right, all to add to the excitement.

The fair had its own smell, a mixture of hot dogs, and onions, candy floss, diesel fumes from the lovely old generators, an odd whiff of perfume from the girls, who loved to hang around the Speedway, and Dodgems. The lads who took your money for the rides always had their suits on on a Saturday night, trying to impress the girls.

The songs I remember the most were, The Platters 'Only You', Frankie Lymon & The Teenagers, 'Why Do Fools Fall in Love,' Bill Haley and His Comets 'Shake, Rake, Rattle and Roll,' Doris Day, "Que Sera Sera," Jonny Ray, 'Just Walking in The Rain,' Pat Boone, 'I'll be Home' and many more.

Geoff and I started going to the pictures on a regular basis, Tuesday and Saturday nights. We either used to call at Bill Doughty's sweet shop, or Elsie Stockdale for our sweets.

Let me tell you about Bill Doughty, his shop was in Market Lane opposite the fish and chip shop, of course not there now, as it was demolished to make way for the Market Lane development in 1965. Bill would sell fizzy pop by the glass, and would measure the drink by eye, holding the glass, and bottle up to his eyes. If he thought he had given you too much, he could pour it back without spilling a drop! The glass always looked like it required a good clean. As you went in the old shop, the bell on the door would 'clang' away, and at the bottom of the door, there was a caster which rolled along the wooden floor. This over the years had left a groove in the floor, and had a sound all on its own. As you closed the door, Bill would come down the two steps from his kitchen to serve you, he would be rubbing his hands together, and peering over his little glasses would say, "Now then boys, what can I get you today? The sherbet fountains have just come in."

We loved them, and still do. The shop had a smell of fusty old things along with sweets, and lemonade, Dandelion and Burdock was a favourite of ours I remember. For our Saturday night supply of sweets, we would go to Elsie Stockdale's shop. She was spotlessly clean, and would sell loose tobacco, as well as first class sweets. So, her shop had a lovely aroma of fresh cut tobacco, sweets, chocolate, and polish! Yes, everywhere was spick & span. At this stage we would be about thirteen to fourteen years old, and she would say, "My, you look smart boys, what is it to be tonight? Raspberry Truffles?"

Geoff and I loved them, as well as Liquorish Comforts, and Coconut Mushrooms. We would spend about half-a-crown, and for this we could buy a 1/4lb of each of those I have mentioned.

The films we saw back then were always good, either thrillers, comedy, romantic. Films like, The Eddie Duchin Story, starring Kim Novak, & Tyrone Power. (Still fantastic) The Glenn Miller Story starring James Stuart, a true story. Dam Busters, Richard Todd, based on a true story about our R.A.F. bombers in the second world war, bombing the German Dams. Other films I remember are Moon Light Bay with Doris Day, Trapeze with Burt Lancaster and Tony Curtis, (brilliant) Hell Drivers with Stanley Baker, Bounty Hunters, Where Eagle's Dare, Norman Wisdom's films (very funny) Mother Riley, he was a bloke, but very funny, dressed up as an old lady.

Geoff and I would drool over Kim Novak, she was stunning! All these films we saw at the Oxford, which was on Newport Street, the old building is still there, but in a poor state. We had Usherettes with torches seeing us to our seats, the cost of entry was from 6d to 2 shillings, and there was always a supporting film on before the interval, which was a Scotland Yard thriller. We loved these, it was always introduced by the voice of Edgar Lustgarten. He had a chilling voice. In the interval, there would be two ladies with ice cream trays, with a little light lighting up a Walls sign. Ice lollies or tubs of ice cream were 6d. So, to sum up, you could go and see a top film, with sweets, ice cream and a bag of chips on the way home for 30p or 6 shillings.

Week day nights we would go to The Star cinema house, this was at the end of the High Street, now it's a hardware store. They would show cowboy films here, and superman, we loved Roy Rogers, Gene Autry, The Durango Kid, and Hop-a-Long Cassidy. The place was a little grotty, like seats well-worn and a few scruffier people would go there, because it was cheaper than 'the Posh Oxford.'

The front seats were called the 'chicken run' or the 'flee pit'. We sat on the front seats, and we could fire peas with our pea shooters at the screen, which was a laugh. Until old Mr Hill would have a walk around with his beady eyes! He was the Cinema Manager. Before the film show on a Saturday afternoon matinee, he would stand in front of the screen, and announce next week's showings.

We would leave the cinema after watching Superman with our coats buttoned round our necks, just with one button, to make it look like a Superman cloak, and our arms out stretched shouting; It's Superman!

In the Summer, we would go fishing down to the old brickyard pits (where The Humber Bridge Country Hotel now stands) on the Humber Bank, which would have Perch, Eels, Roach, and other fresh water fish.

We would walk in the warm mud when the tide was out, and the lovely smell of the Humber bank was something I hadn't experienced before. We would go quite a lot and also had some fun times at the old cement works. Writing about fishing reminds me of the miles we used to cycle. It was no wonder we were all skinny.

In the High Street at Barton, there was an Ice Cream Parlour called Havercrofts, they made their own Ice Cream, it was delicious! Friday afternoons were always busy with shoppers, the lady shoppers would call, and have a chat, along with an Ice Cream. Mr Havercroft had a large three-wheel peddle trike, it had a lovely canopy over the front of it with the Havercroft name on where the Ice Cream was sold. This was served up into either cornets 1d to 6d, (2.5p), a wafer sandwich or tubs. As he would peddle his trike around the estate where we lived, he would ring his bell to get your attention. There were other Ice Cream shops in Barton, but Havercroft's was the best.

The shops back then were all busy, and well stocked, there were many grocery shops providing people with anything they wanted from one end of the town, to the other. Barton had many shops and garages back then to provide customers with anything they wanted, from a reel of cotton to a brand-new car.

On Thursday afternoon, it was half day closing for all general shops, and Barton was like a ghost town. The only trading places open were garages, and we had three of those. I remember, I could leave our house in 14 Harrowdyke, sit on my trolley, and because it was all downhill, I could reach The Wheatsheaf Pub.

It was common to see a group of cows walking down the main road, heading for Hoodless' Farm near the Wheatsheaf. Mr Hoodless would be on his bike, with a stick keeping them in order, (and I have to say, there was shit everywhere) it always amazed us, the cows could walk and shit at the same time! All this took place every day, morning and night, as cows require milking twice a day.

We had four or five little farms dotted around the town back then, so seeing cows walking down the road with farmer and dog was normal. Geoff and I would ride around Barton after tea when it was dark with our new bikes, and miller dynamo lighting systems lighting the whole street up.

The smell of the fish and chip shops, and people stoking their coal fires up, all those smells were wonderful. Eating chips when it was a frosty night was great; they always tasted so good, with plenty of salt and vinegar and grease piling up on your fingers with the cold, all added to the pleasure.

On Sunday nights in the winter, Geoff and I would go back to our house, and watch Sunday Night at The London Palladium. We had just had the telly changed to receive ITV in 1954, it was rented, no one bought them back then, and when we first saw the adds, we loved it. There was always a star act on, Frankie Vaughn, Jonny Ray, Pat Boone, Guy Mitchel, David Whitfield, Bill Haley and His Comets, Liberace the Pianist, Slim Whitman once, and many more. Gran would do 'bread & dripping' and a pot of tea, then she would bring out a homemade jam tart or two. She always used to feed us, but because we were biking everywhere we were still skinny.

In the Summer Sunday nights, we would go on the bus to Scunthorpe to see a film at the A.B.C. Sadly now long gone, but it was a very nice place. One film I remember was called A Summer Place staring the lovely Sandra Dee, a wonderful film with the music of Percy Faith and his Orchestra, playing the theme song throughout the film.

I remember once on the way home, Geoff and I were upstairs on the bus, when it stopped for the Inspector to get on. I had been fiddling with my ticket, and it was in bits on the floor. He came upstairs checking all tickets. Geoff says, "Looks like you are going to have to pay again." I pointed to the wrecked ticket. "That will be 'four-bob' then lad!" said the Inspector smugly. (Geoff remembers this to this day) with him having his all intact. Ah good memories.

I had already started taking notice of girls. One girl I remember was June Foster. She lived three streets away from us, and went to music lessons, so I would bike past her at the time she would be walking down the street just to say hello. I never took her out, but she would give me a lovely smile, and say hello back. June later dated my good friend Dave Story who loved her very much, but it didn't work out for them and June went to live in Sheffield and married. She came back to Barton, and I was lucky enough to see her in Summer 2014. She was walking in the town when I was lettering a shop. She saw my name on the van and stopped to say hello, she still has the lovely smile. Of course, she is a little older but still so sweet.

Then there was Gillian Topps, she was in my class the last two years at school. Pretty girl, but just a school crush, we used to smile at one another.

I also sent the odd love letters, but that was it. She is now Mrs Hardy, and lives on Habrough Road. Immingham. We have always been friends though, Malc Hardy is her brother-in-law.

In the Winter when the snow came, Geoff and I would take our sledges to green pits. This was an old redundant quarry on Barrow Road. Over the years it had grassed over, and was ideal when covered with snow. It had natural slopes, and small hills, there was one which was a curving steep slope leading to a double hump. It was nick-named 'Camel's Hump', then there was 'Break Neck,' a steep hill that took you across the whole quarry, the whole area was just brilliant. I remember we used to go there after tea with lamps on our sledges, and called at the chip shop on the way home. It was always exciting when it snowed (and it always did!)

Now the Bereton School is built on the whole area, and green pits is long gone, but what a great childhood memory, and it cost nothing.

In those days when the Fox Hunt season started, the head master of the school would arrange for all the seniors to go to the market place where the Hunt had gathered with the hounds. I remember thinking what a lovely sight.

All the main huntsmen would be in red coats sat on the beautiful horses, and we would see them take the sherry; wish everyone well in the ride. Then the bugle blower would sound the cry, and off they went. This would be accepted as the norm, no protesters, or banners, thing was back then, we didn't know how good we were having it.

The year was 1956, my school days were coming to an end, and the last class I was in was Brian "killer" Creasy's. This guy was ex-army, and did he put us through it, or what! That's where his nick name came from. If he caught any of the lads messing about, he would give us the slipper, (and boy did it hurt).

We had a class reunion at Providence House quite a long time ago, Brian (Mr Creasy) was there to meet us and have a chat. He brought us photos of our old classes to view, and gave me the opportunity to thank him for how he taught us. I grew up thinking what a great teacher he was, and how he instilled such respect.

Brian is sadly now deceased, but Geoff and I attended his funeral and St Mary's Church was full for him which speaks volumes about the legacy he has left.

Regarding my education, I did enough to get by but I was always told; Mervin could do so much better if he tried harder, but I couldn't wait to leave, and never wanted to go back either.

So, Christmas came 1956, and I finished my days at Providence House, that was the over spill school. Bereton opened the following year built on our beloved 'green pits.'

My school report was simple, but encouraging;

To whom it may concern,

Mervin Dove is a pleasant, happy lad who shows evidence of developing into an extremely good worker.

Patient, reliable and trustworthy to the extreme, his work has been stamped by personal effort and integrity, and his progress has been steady. He is well mannered, he takes pride in his appearance and I have pleasure in recommending him.

Headmaster - J. Taylor.

Having left school, I went straight down to Eagle House, where Jack Leaning lived with his wife and Violet. Jack was Pop's old boss and still visited our house in Barton for a chat. On answering the door to me, I asked him for a job on his farm were Pop worked, and of course he said yes.

He didn't want to see my school report, and I so wanted him to ask for it.

Gran's Scrambled Egg Sandwiches

I remember my first day at work. Gran got up at 6.15am for me to start work at 7am. It was a ten-minute bike ride to the farm, Glebe Farm was on the left going to Barrow, sadly the farm has long gone, and The Options Specialist School has been built on the land now.

I remember before we moved to Barton, I used to bike down from Barrow Mere to Glebe Farm and walk through three fields to reach my good friend Stuart James' house. Unfortunately, you had to negotiate a very narrow bridge over a deep dyke. The bridge was green and slimy, scary I'm thinking now, but once there we used to have some fun times and I remember his lovely mum fussing over me giving me drinks and something to eat. I also remember walking home again at dusk hearing the curlews calling and the dim lights of Glebe Farm over the fields where I was heading. It was always dark when I arrived home and Gran would be pleased to see me although covered with mud from the long trek.

Anyway, Gran had bought me a new lunch box and flask for my first day. I had been to Scunthorpe, and bought a lunch bag to carry them in. All the workers had these; it was part of the 1950's work kit. So that morning Gran packed me up scrambled egg sandwiches (with real butter), and angel cake with coffee in my new flask. I couldn't wait to get to work.

It was chucking it down with rain, and I had a heavy ex-army top coat on with my cap, and wellingtons. When I got to the farm, yes, I was already wet. We all met in the old horse stables and left our bikes there too. When I pushed my bike through the old door, I saw a shadowy figure in the corner smoking a fag. As it was still a bit dark, I couldn't see who it was.

Anyway, a voice said, "Are you Mervin?"

"Yes," I said.

He said, "I'm Ray Hewitt," (later in my working life, Ray and I worked together again). Also working on the farm in those days were, Pete Sanderson, Jack, Pete's brother (deceased), Pete Osgerby, my mentor, but sadly also deceased, he was my hero, a top tractor driver who taught me how to handle a tractor, and reverse a four-wheel trailer.

Anyway, that morning Norman the boss' son came into the stable to give us our orders for the day. Norman told me to go with Ray, his job was to lead cattle food out of the fields where Fodder Beet, Mangolds, and Cale were grown. He had an old Fordson Major tractor with a two-wheel trailer. It was still a bit dark when we went into the old shed where the tractor was. This had to be hand started. The smell of the paraffin exhaust fumes from the tractor starting up are still with me, I loved it. There I was wet with the rain, but excited about working, and Ray was so funny, a good laugh all day.

At 8.30am it was breakfast time, this was spent in Violet's little den which was in the dairy. We all sat round eating our sandwiches and chatting. Gran's scrambled egg was lovely, I ate all six with angel cake and coffee, at 8.50am a guy called Ray Coupland would call with his milk lorry and collect the milk which was in churns waiting outside the dairy. He would come in for a cup of tea, and discuss football with the lads. Sometimes Violet would be cooking meat on her gas stove for the dogs in the same place, but the meat had gone off. That bloody smell is still with me too, it was so heavy and hung around. Later, the lads got her to boil it while we were out, that was a blessing I'll tell you.

Pulling the root food out of the ground was done no matter what the weather, so on a frosty morning with white frost on the leaves your hands went a bit numb, but you got used to it.

Twelve o'clock came, and off we biked home to dinner, Gran had it ready always, and Pop wanted to know everything that I had been doing. Dinner over, I biked back to work to repeat what Ray and I had been doing in the morning. At four o'clock Ray and I started feeding the stock, this was done by filling wire baskets which when full weighed about three stone (me at fifteen years old!) I grew up quickly, not wanting the boss to think I couldn't do it. My weekly wage then was £3.10s, 45 hours per week Monday to Saturday lunch time.

I do know that when Norman the boss asked Ray how I was doing, he always said I was doing well, and he encouraged me. When we were in the crew yard to feed the cattle, they would come around us sniffing and pushing to get to the food, it was hard work at my age trying to walk on the straw. The food was put into troughs called Tumbrils, whilst doing this it was dark, there were a few lights but not like we have today.

Back then in a Winter the Thrashing Set would arrive in the yard, this was a contractor called Tom Heblewhite, and son Doug. It was my job as the junior member to carry the chaff from the machine (chaff is the husk from the corn) A filthy dusty job, I had to carry it across the yard into the chaff house. I had to be quick too, because the machine would soon clog up, and I would be told off! Talking about this memory now reminds me we didn't wear dusk masks, or any protection from the massive belt that drove the machine from the tractor. A farm yard in those days was full of hazards which we didn't see but do today, however the job always got done.

Ten o'clock came, and it was cup of tea time. Violet would have the tea ready for us all in a big white enamel milk bucket. We would stand in the barn, and drink the tea, each one dipping a mug into the bucket washing the dust down as the men said. Most of them smoked too, so it was their chance to have a quick fag. Then ten minutes later and back to it. The chaff I handled was used for mixing with cattle feed. The thrashing contractors would visit our farm six or seven times through the winter months, something I dreaded because it meant the chaff hole for me.

At the end of January, the lambing season would start; all three hundred ewes had to be walked on the main road to Top Farm. This was situated off Ferriby Road outside of Barton in a valley, the chap in charge was called Sid Nott, he was a nice friendly man and a good shepherd. That first lambing time I spent with him, helping to lamb the sheep, feed them and build sheep pens with bales. I loved to see the lambs develop and grow, then gang up and run about kicking their legs in the air.

At the end of the lambing season, Spring was on its way, and it was a lovely time. On the way down to the farm, the daffodils had come out and it was a lovely sight. I went back to Glebe Farm, and by then it was time to drill the corn. I got teamed up with Pete Osgerby, (my mentor). It was my job to ride on the back of the drill to make sure the corn was running freely into the land. Pete could drive across a field as straight as tram lines, I loved this job, he made it really interesting. He always had a smile on his face, and any tractor task was just so easy for him, little did he know, in my tractor driving future as I got older and moved on to other employment, he played a big part in my skills as a confident tractor driver.

I remember when the potatoes were planted; we would sit on the back of a potato planter and plant them in the perfect straight rows that Pete had made with his ridging plough. There would be three of us sat on the machine, and we would put the spuds in cups as they came around on a dish, day in day out, for two weeks.

Another job on the farm was mucking out the crew yard, this was interesting, the smell of all the winter manure was a bit intoxicating to say the least. This job was carried out in early summer, so the flies were very excited to be there with us. We would have breakfast 8.30am and never dream of washing our hands, yes eating our sandwiches with crew yard shit on your hands. But what makes me smile now is that we always swilled our boots off before we went into Violets den.

After that task was complete, the sugar beet required 'singling', this was done on piece work, you didn't get paid by the week as normal, but by the acre. As far as I can remember back then it was about £6. per acre, and it was possible to do one and a half acre per week (60hr). So, compared to the weekly wage of £5.80p for an adult, you could earn some real money. I remember back then my first £5. note in my wage packet, they were large white ones with black lettering. (Double the size of today).

After the sugar beet, it was hay time (cattle food), this was a lovely time, the smell of the freshly cut hay in the fields with the summer sun on it was amazing, and still is. I still stop when I can if there is a freshly cut hay field, just to take in the lovely smell. Hay was bailed, loaded on a tractor and trailer, and then stacked in the farm yard for the winter food.

After the hay time, came harvesting the corn. I would be with Pete through the harvest time, he was in charge of the combine harvester, it was what you called a bag combine. Back then combines were in their infant days; my job was to change the bags over as they filled up with corn. This was done on a platform attached to the combine; the sacks weighed about sixteen stone, and remember I was only fifteen years old. You grew up quickly in those days.

I would slide the sacks down a shoot and try and keep them in a line across the field. Later the sacks would be collected with a loader on the front of a tractor and put on a trailer, finally took to the granary store. Harvest back then was very hard work compared with today's procedure, twelve hours per day was the normal day in harvest time. We went home tired and slept well.

Harvest time over, it was then potato lifting time. A gang of women would arrive on the back of our lorry driven by Pete. I wonder what the safety officer would have to say now about the 'bus service' back then. The women would wait in the Barton Market Place at 8.30am for Pete with his lorry, which had boxes on the back for them to sit on (no seat belts then). There would be a little ladder for the women to climb on the back, then off to the farm for a 'day's spud picking,' as they called it.

My task was to be with the men emptying the potato baskets into the trailers the women had filled, the potatoes were put in a large long pile called a clamp or pie at the end of the field, then covered with straw, and soil. Later they would be sold to a potato merchant after being riddled and bagged into eight stone sacks for the customers.

I remember one lunch time I got back early, and as I walked near the women who were just finishing their lunch time, Norman the boss said; "Wait here Merv, they won't have 'squeezed their lemons' yet." I'm thinking what's he talking about? How could anybody want to have bitter lemon? Then he explained that it meant they hadn't had a 'wee' yet. I still think what a strange saying, never heard it since that day, but I remember it well.

I also remember the woman were full of banter, and always had a laugh with the men, and pulled my leg regarding the females. You could say I quickly learned a lot about the 'birds and the bees.' Potato harvest done.

The Autumn was well on the way now, and sugar beet harvest was about to begin. Back in those days the sugar beet was delivered to Brigg Sugar Beet Factory, which went through processing machines to produce sugar. The by-product was sugar beet pulp, this was animal food, and once or twice through the season, our lorry (driven by Pete) would come back with a load which would be stacked in the barn for the animal feed. Pete would drive the tractor pulling the beet lifting machine, the beet would then be lifted in the tractor and trailer which was running alongside the lifting machine, then tipped in a big heap at the edge of the field. The sugar beet harvest would last until late January. I had now done my first year, and loved it.

At this time, a lad called Trevor Richardson started work with me, we had some damn good laughs. Trev was a good worker, and very witty, making jokes about the men and Violet. No need to expand on that, but it was funny at the time as she never had a male companion. Just the oversized wellingtons.

In my second year at Leanings I got to drive the tractor a bit more, this was an exciting time for me, and having Pete to learn from made it extra good. My first task was harrowing, to explain this, it was dragging five big frames with big forks on, and it brakes the land up ready for the corn drill to do its job.

Today that's all gone, now they have a cultivator which is much quicker and cost effective. But I knew I would never be a regular tractor driver if I stayed at Leanings, so I started looking in The Lincolnshire Times, which was a local paper advertising jobs etc. This paper now is long gone, sad really because everybody I have talked to loved it.

Tractors & Coach Trips

So, it was January 1959, and I was looking in the paper and there it was; "Tractor Driver" required, full pay for successful applicant, Jack Andrew & Sons Park Farm Barton. So, I was on my bike to Grange Farm where Mr Andrew lived. All the way up Ferriby Road about three miles then across two fields on a track, I knocked on the door and a well-rounded man answered.

"Now then boy, who are you?"

After explaining that I was applying for the tractor driving job, his reply was "Aw I see, weer ah ya working now?"

(This was still on the door step).

After telling him where I was working, he said,

"Right then, when do ya want to get started?"

Still on the door step, with the wind blowing, I said "In a week I think."

"Hey that'll do lad."

I thanked him and as I rode away, he shouted, "What did ya say ya name was?"

I shouted my name and he nodded. I was so excited, feeling the wind behind me downhill back to

Barton, I couldn't wait to tell Gran and Pop. Having told them, Pop said "Well if yar on more money boy, ya can save a bit!"

Makes sense talking about it now, but saving wasn't on my mind back then. Pop was a plain talker, said what he thought; never left you wondering what he meant.

I remember the following week dragged on, and I couldn't wait to leave the following Saturday, I even checked the Lincolnshire Times when I got home to see if the job advert had been removed, which of course it had.

Monday morning finally came, up like a lark and Gran had got me all packed with flask and scrambled egg sandwiches, and angel cake of course. Five-minute bike ride and I was there, greeted with Bill Thew.

"Good morning *Melvin*." He always called me that.

At the farm that morning I also met the other workers, Bob Broughton, he was a tractor driver, and Ernie Holden. Finally, Alf Needler, he was a good guy, good worker and I use to make him laugh with some of the things I got up to. Sadly he is now deceased.

At the other farm, Barton Grange, there were other workers; Tom Taylor, Harold Dannart, and Ernie Wright. Ralph was at school with him and because he seemed clever and bossy, Ralph nicknamed him "SARG" (short for Sergeant). Anyway, Ralph told me about Ernie and said; "When you see Ernie just say; now then Sarg."

So, I did. Of course, he was annoyed, and said, "Who told you to say that?" From then on, I often called him that just for a laugh.

So, that day I started work at Andrews, up walks the foreman George Canty. He was a good man, he greeted us all with a good morning and smile.

"Naw then you'll be Merv," he said looking at me. There were not many handshakes in them days.

"Have you been to plough before then mate?"

"Yes, just a little," I said.

"Awh well ya better go and get that Fordson over in that shed, n go down lane Second Field on left, and get going ploughing then."

Well, excited like you wouldn't believe, I started the tractor up, backed out the shed and off I went with my own tractor to plough. As I dropped the plough into the land it was a wonderful feeling, me in charge of this big tractor and the first diesel engine I had driven, the smell of the engine fumes from the exhaust mixed with the lovely smell of the freshly turned soil from the plough, and a few seagulls following. I was loving it.

Breakfast time soon came and it was back to the yard. I sat with the other men in a little hut. Bob smoking his pipe afterwards, and talking about how good he was at ploughing soon made me get back to my ploughing.

Geoff, at this point, was still working for a farmer just down the road from where I was working, at Val Nettleton's Barton Hill Farm and enjoying it like me.

Not many tractors had cabs back then, so you were open to getting wet, cold, and whatever the weather was you just got on with it. Thrashing came around on this farm too, but instead of carrying the light chaff, it was my job to carry the corn which was sixteen stone. This was lifted to shoulder height with a Hicking Barrow, a contraption that you had to wind up with the sack on it, so you could then drop it across your shoulders to carry it into the granary about thirty yards away then up the stairs to store it. This procedure was every ten minutes, starting work at 7am to 5pm, having our tea breaks and dinner time of course, but as I am writing about the thrashing days, I can't believe I did this, and for a wage of £5.12.6d per week, but that was a good wage for me, not even eighteen years old.

I stayed at Andrews eighteen months doing everything there was to be done with a tractor. I could reverse a four-wheel trailer off the road just outside the farm straight into the crew yard in one go, having been shown how to do this by my mentor Pete from my first job. Now this used to really annoy old Ernie Holden, because before I arrived at the farm, the previous tractor driver was useless, and it took him thirty minutes at least to reverse in, giving Ernie longer for his smoke break.

One Saturday morning, George told me and Bill 'gath up' (feeding the bullocks in the crew yard). We had a large fork that would hold two bales of straw at one time. Walking with this load on your back in the crew yard was hard work. Bill is working away with the fork when I said, "I bet you can't carry three Bill."

Of course he said, "Who me? I'll show you *Melvin.*"

Well you should have seen him; two bales on the fork and one under his arm struggling and grunting, but I have to say he did it. Poor old Bill always used to take the bait and we had many laughs at his expense.

It was during this time that my sister Pearl started organizing coach trips. She was very good at this, running around collecting money from people who were going on the trip.

The year would be 1958/59 and I recall one trip going to see The Everly Brothers, who were visiting the UK for the first time. The trip was to The Gaumont at Doncaster.

Mick Smaller owned the coach, a well-built guy who was a very good driver. The coach was always full thanks to Pearl.

The Everlys were fantastic, I still have the programme. The backing group for them were The Crickets, Buddy Holly's group. He had just recently been killed in a light aircraft along with Ritchie Valens and The Big Bopper.

Halfway through the concert they said they had a new song, and introduced Cathy's Clown. I have seen many concerts, but that one ranks at the top for me.

On the way home that November night it was pouring with rain. Now Geoff and I had noticed Linda Grimbleby on the coach. This girl was absolutely stunning, with long black hair and the prettiest face ever. She had a boyfriend but this night she was with a girlfriend. When the coach stopped at Ferriby Road corner in Barton to let her off, as she passed our seat she leaned over and said to me, "Are you walking me home Merv?"

I turned to Linda and said "Yes."

As we walked with arms around one another and rain finding its way into everywhere it could, we turned into her passage which linked the little terrace houses where she lived with her Mam. (The Lidl shop stands there now). She turned around quickly, and with her lush lips she gave me the best kiss ever, with the rain running down our faces. It lasted forever. We said good night and I walked home in the rain with the Everly Bros ringing in my ears, thinking of that magical moment with Linda. She was back with her boyfriend after that, I should have asked her out but I didn't. She always gave me a lovely smile when I saw her though. I have often wondered what would have happened if I had taken it further.

But I have the special memory. I have no idea where she is today, all I know is she went away to live down south and left me with that special moment in my teens.

About this time in my life, Ben and I bought a car; A Standard Series 8 1939 model. We paid £20 for it, a fair bit of money back then. I began learning to drive in this with Ralph. He would turn up every Sunday morning to take me out for a drive. Usually we would go up Caistor Road out of Barton, and head for

Kirmington past the old airport which was derelict after the war. Of course, it's now Humberside Airport.

We used to continue up to Grasby to see Aunty Elsie and Uncle Bert. Auntie Elsie was Pop's youngest sister and chose not to have children; she would tell you what she thought to the point of being rude. She was bed ridden with ulcers on her legs, and I remember seeing her in bed propped up on pillows. When she saw me with my hair style and tight trousers she said "Well Merv you look a sight, what the hell have you got on?" I hadn't seen her for a while and forgot how harsh she could be. I just laughed it off.

Anyway, one Sunday morning we got to Grasby Bottom on the way to see her again, when the old car broke down. Ralph said; "I think the battery has blown up." Well it had, right near a sugar beet heap, and it was freezing too. But our luck was in as a guy on a motorbike came by and asked if we required help. Having told him what had happened, he went to the nearest garage, which was at Kealby. They eventually came out to us, and towed us back to the garage. That morning for some reason I had all my money on me. The new battery and tow in, on a Sunday remember, cost nearly £20, just about what we paid for the car. Now back then there weren't many phones, not in our family anyway. So, poor Marjorie must have been worried sick about Ralph, as it was well after 2pm when we got back. We should have been back for midday.

So, after explaining to Ben what had happened, and what it had cost me, I'm asking him for half the cost.

"How much?! You would have done better giving them the car."

Pop chimes in; "Pay up and stop moaning!" Back then Ben's money used to end up in the pub, so I always seemed to have more money than him. It took him a long time to get over that one.

We traded that car in at a garage in Ferriby Sluice; we got a Morris 12 with a lovely shine, dark green and black. The only problem was that the steering had a load of play in it, so it was hard for me to keep it going straight up the road. The chassis was rotten, and the suspension went through the floor. Back then there were no MOT's until 1960, so you could buy some junk. This one we had bought was on H.P.

Ben said; "We arn't paying anymore for this damn thing boy," so we cut our losses and took it back, and left it on their garage front. That was the end of it.

It was about this time I met a girl called Jean Dixon who lived in Barrow. I would bike over to see her. She was a lovely girl who I saw for several weeks. I remember biking home after seeing her and smelling her makeup, which was lovely. I remember we both liked Eddie Cochran, a young rock and roll singer. Jean had a Danset record player and she would sit on it while it played which was quite funny. We had some fun moments but it wasn't to be and we went our separate ways, I sometimes see Jean today in or around Barton and she is still as lovely as ever and it is always a pleasure to see her.

Pearl organized many bus trips, and we saw stars like; Cliff Richard, Craig Douglas, Helen Shapiro, Frankie Vaughn, Emile Ford, Lonnie Donegan, and many more. Some of these we saw at the London Palladium, for weekends away.

One trip Pearl did was a bus load of us to Scarborough. Geoff and I got the front seat next to the driver Arthur Farr. Arthur was a good driver and the bus a Bedford Duple, in its day a lovely bus. I remember we hit a thunder storm halfway there, as we stopped for a tea break it had just about stopped. The cafe car park was flooded. We arrived in Scarborough about 11am, back in the early fifties there weren't any motorways, so route was; from Barton to Scunthorpe, always through the town centres of course, then Keadby Bridge and onto Thorne, after that Goole and the old Boothferry Bridge. Then onto Scarborough through various towns and villages. It was a three and a quarter hour journey. We had lovely fish and chips for dinner, I know they were good but I can't remember where it was.

Later, Geoff and I strolled round the prom; it was there we came across this little jeweller's shop. In the window was a silver Saint Christopher that caught my eye. I went in to take a closer look, the price was £1.1s. or back then a guinea. I liked it and bought it. Yes, I still wear it, and have done from that day, so it must be fifty-six years old or more. But talking about it now, it seems just a few years ago. How the time goes.

Pearl did many more trips for us; like when we went for the day to Cadwell Park near Louth. I remember it was always lovely weather, we would sit on the grass with sandwiches, and there was a van there selling fish and chips. These were pre-cooked at a fish shop in Louth, then wrapped up in newspaper into fish and chips parcels sold at 2s.6p each = 12.5p, and we thought they were expensive, because at Barton the same was 1s.9p = 8p.

It was at this time when I met a good friend, Mick (Custard) Kirkby. He came to work at Andrew's farm for a while, we used to have a laugh every day. Mick was a good man and worker, and in later years on the road tankers when I worked for Fina, Mick worked for Shell. Sadly, we lost Mick. He was only a young man in his early fifties, but my memories of him are still alive. His lovely wife Janet still lives on her own, occasionally I see her whilst out and it's always a pleasure but of course I know she has never got over him. Why would you?

The year would be 1959 and Geoff and I had heard there was some jobs going at Barton Maltkin's, this was a place where the process was to turn barley corn into Malt which went to the Brewers for making Beer. The attraction to work there was money. We both secured a job there in the barley gang which gave us £3. a week more.

Let me tell you about the interview for the job. The boss' name was Harry Dean, a keen gardener as we found out at the interview one late spring night. The appointment time and place came from our neighbour in Harrowdyke where I lived.

Ernie worked as a Maltser (top job) and said Harry wants to see you tonight at his house in Westfield Road. So, I biked up to Geoff's and we went to see Harry that night. The interview was carried out in his garden! We spoke about gardening and farming. He kept telling us because we were used to farm work, this job wasn't for us really, and we would never settle working inside. We of course said we would, so he said okay and asked us when we could start. A week's time was agreed and that was the 'interview' in the garden.

Back then you could walk out of one job straight into another one; I had many interviews like that one.

So, we both started work at Barton Maltkins. It was a lovely Spring morning and there we were in this enormous building, no tractors, no blue skies, no fresh air, no farm yard smells or tractor fumes, just dust and barley and more barley. But we settled in and started to enjoy being there, a good gang of lads to work with too. Geoff and I used to sit with a bloke called Bert Warriner who could tell the biggest lies you ever heard. I would feed him with a few yarns so he would expand on it. One story he used to tell us was that him and his wife would go out on their Tandem Bike on Sunday afternoons, and do about 100 miles. So, I said;

(just to feed him) bet you could reach about 45 to 50 miles an hour Bert!

"Yes," he said, "Quite easily if it was a back wind." I thought yeah right! If a vehicle was towing you! Geoff had a job keeping from laughing sometimes, because some of the rubbish that came out his mouth (with my help) was amazing, how he made it up, we never knew.

An old friend of mine John McIntyre had worked there before us, and he also had experienced Bert with his tall stories. So, John bought a liar's licence from a joke shop, and put it up on the mess room wall near where Bert sat. He never made a comment about it then, or when we asked him about it. We think he was proud of it and it probably inspired him.

It was at this point in my life that Geoff and I started learning to drive with a proper school of motoring in Brigg. We would travel there on the bus on Saturday afternoons. We would meet the teacher with his car in Cary Lane. The car was a new Standard 10 and lovely to drive. I remember it was 15 shillings a lesson, which would be 75p. This went on for a few weeks until he told me to put in for my test, saying that I was ready. I went on to pass first time.

I remember the songs at that time; Good Timing by Jimmy Jones, Bobby Darrin Dream Lover, Elvis, All Shook Up, Cliff Richard, Living Doll, and many more.

After several weeks working at Barton Maltkins, one day Bob the barley gang charge hand asked Geoff and I if we would like overtime 'throwing off malt'. This job was hot and filthy. Malt was the final product after barley (which had shoots on) had been cooked in a giant kiln. The heat was like being cooked in an oven Gas Mark 8. It was our job to load our wheel barrows and tip it in the big hopper at the end of the kiln. We worked only in shorts and special shoes supplied by the firm; it was this job that tipped me over the edge and rekindled an urge to go back to the farm. Geoff stayed a little longer.

I went back to Andrews, this was just before harvest started, so I had been at The Maltkins for nearly three months. It is now sadly all gone. A nature reserve has taken its place.

I have to say it was a pleasure to be back on the farm, breathing in the lovely fresh air, and looking forward to a few bus trips with Geoff which my sister Pearl organized.

These were to London. We would leave Friday night from Barton Market Place about 11pm. It was exciting going to the big city and travelling through the night, stopping off at Jacks Hill Cafe just fifteen miles away from London. I remember eating egg and chips at 5am but I don't remember feeling tired.

On this trip, we went to see Cliff Richard at the Palladium. Des O'Connor was the compare I remember, only a young bloke then. On the Sunday, I went with Pearl on a Thames river trip with some other people, and I remember having my photo taken which I still have.

Dances & Black Suede Shoes

After that coach trip, sadly Geoff and I parted company for some time, I think maybe his time had come to do his own thing, and at that time or soon after he met Gillian his wife now of many years. I am pleased to say we have been back together as good friends for many years of which I value and the four of us get together on a regular basis.

Soon after, my social life began to change. I was still working at Park Farm (Andrews). Autumn was on its way. I started knocking about with a lad Hugh Tunbridge, who I had known since we were young lads. He was lead singer in the local rock-n-roll band which used to play the local dance halls. The first night I went with him was to the Crosby Hotel at Scunthorpe which was brilliant. There were plenty of girls to dance with, but no one special. There were many nights like that, all good venues in Barton, Brigg, Wootton, Barrow, Goxhill, Caistor and Immingham, which was one of the best ones.

Dress style was drain pipes and plenty of time in front of the mirror. One Saturday afternoon, I went to Kenny Milson's shop to see what he had in.

"Now then Mr Taylor, how are you?" he asked with his trilby hat and permanent grin. I bought some narrow black jeans, zip jacket to match, and a red shirt. I already had my black suede shoes and white socks, the collar on the red shirt was stiff to stand up. Of course, Pop wasn't too impressed.

Whilst working at Andrew's farm I had become good friends with John, the son of the boss. He was carefree and loved the girls company. He used to drive around in a big car, Austin Sheerline then later Riley Pathfinder, both lovely cars, vintage now. He used to cruise around Barton, and the villages visiting all the dances. One Saturday lunchtime just as I was finishing to go home, he came in the yard and asked if I wanted to go to Goxhill dance. I agreed and was picked up in the Market Place that night all dressed up with hair perfect, John rolls up in his Austin Sheerline, which was on the same scale as a Bentley. The radio was tuned in to Radio Luxembourg, and I remember The Everlys were on singing 'Till I Kissed Ya.' It was fading in and out because of the signal, but to have a radio in a car was something, I can tell you.

So off we went to Goxhill dance, the Rock-n-Roll band was from Brigg, and very good. Just to experience the music and dancing back then was great. I just sort of jived straight away and as I progressed with different girls I started putting in fancy moves that I picked up from watching the new series Six-Five Special Rock-n-Roll Show on telly Saturday teatimes.

It was that night I met Pam Clayton. I asked her to dance and was with her for the rest of the night. She had the prettiest eyes with the longest eyelashes, and was very attractive. At five feet two, she was stunning, with a smile to melt you. Her manner was quiet and gentile, and I was thinking, God, is this love?

The kiss good night was even better, I didn't want to leave her, and she didn't want to leave me, but John was getting impatient so we said good night, and I promised to see her the following weekend at Barton Drill Hall. But the following weekend came and I went to The Café Dancent at Cleethorpes with Hugh and the lads, which I am certainly not proud to have done. Along with our Rock-n-Roll band, there that night was Shane Fenton and The Fentones, (also known as Alvin Stardust, sadly now deceased).

That place was fantastic just across from the Winter Gardens, all sadly pulled down and gone, lovely memories though.

The following Saturday came and Barton dance was on again at the Drill Hall, (now sadly pulled down too). The band that played there most Saturdays was Harold Johnson, who was the pianist, the trumpet player was Arthur Teasdale, who was married to my Auntie Mary. The band also had a drummer and clarinet player, and a friend of mine Tich Paul was the singer. He went on to be lead singer with The Echo's.

The Drill Hall was fantastic, it had a coffee bar upstairs where we would go and have a chat over a cup of coffee, about the latest songs that had played on Juke Box Jury which was on Saturday tea time. The signature tune played on that show was called 'Hit and Miss,' and the band used to play this, it was great to jive to.

Pam was there and I said a big 'sorry' and we got together. She was lovely with her sparkling eyes and gorgeous smile. We danced all night and I escorted her to her bus kissing her good night and arranging to see her in the week. This went on for a few months.

A friend of mine, Jeff Elm, who was seeing another girl at Goxhill (now married to her and in New Zealand) went with me on the train from Barton at 7.40pm arriving 8.05pm, leaving at 9.20pm. We would go for a walk, hold hands, kiss and that was it. I asked her age, and when she said fifteen years old, I thought she was young. Anyway, we drifted apart; I think Pam thought I was a bit too old for her at eighteen years old.

It would be about this time when I started going around with Alan Stamp, (top man) Dave Story, and Roy (Spam) Stanford, who was lead guitarist with The Echo's. We had some fantastic nights out, always going to Immingham Tin Mission Hut for Thursday Night Rock N Roll, Wootton Village Hall for the Friday night dance, Brigg Corn Exchange Saturday night (one a month) and many more.

I particularly remember when we went to Grimsby, we would turn into Freeman Street at night from Riby Square, and the lights on all the shops would look so great. I would always say to the lads "Wow look at the lights," to hear them say "Here he goes again!" Lovely memories though. You see back then there were no shutters at the windows and all the shops were occupied, so this helped the shop owners to display their wares and allow people to stroll the streets at night window shopping, which was lovely!

It was Winter and I was still at Andrews, I was ploughing in a very muddy field. The tractor kept getting stuck, and I had to keep asking the foreman to tow me out of the bog. Well he started blaming me for this and said he would have to send someone else if I couldn't cope with the conditions. So, what did I do? Yes, I told him to stick his job and walked off there and then! His son tried talking me into staying, but my mind was made up, it was time to move on and that was the end of my farming days.

My next job was to be at a contracting firm called Clugstons at Scunthorpe. I had started looking at lorry driving and this firm was advertising for one. Well I didn't get it but was offered a labouring job working for them on the steel works at £6. a week. It was far more than farm work, but what a shock to the system this was! Up at 5.30am to catch the bus in the market place at 6.20am to start work for 7.30am. My task was shovelling rock bits into a large bucket that the crane lifted up when full, and then do it all over again. There were about forty blokes working there then. We were digging the foundations for a new coking plant which was being built. This job was in the Winter months.

Alan Stamp, my old mate, asked me if I could go with him to Grimsby because his driving test was due. I agreed having had permission to have the day off. So off we went to Grimsby for Alan's test, he had his own car an Austin A40 Devon model, a few years old but in good 'nick' as we used to say. Alan didn't pass that day, but we went to a Chinese Restaurant in Freeman Street, this was one of the few back then. Now I wouldn't have ever gone in, because I was a faddy eater. Anyway, I had a mushroom omelette with chips and peas, and I have to say it was good. Alan tucked into a curry with rice, but just the smell was awful for me. On our way home I felt ill, and had the flu coming on. When I got home I went straight to bed rendering me two more days off without permission.

It was on the Friday night when I was still recovering in bed (this bout of flu was a bad one), when Ben came up stairs to me with my P45 in his hand.

"You have lost your job mate," he said. Although work had been informed they still finished me for being away from the job. I wasn't too bothered about not going to that place anymore, and it was then that my lorry driving days were about to start.

Stamp & Son Builders on Brigg Road in Barton was advertising for a Labourer/Lorry Driver. It was the beginning of Spring 1960 and a beautiful morning. I said to Gran at breakfast; I think I will go and see about that driving job at Stamps, so off I went. It was like talking to a pair of Victorian Gentlemen when I arrived. I was invited in the office but not to sit down. Jack Stamp was the boss and his secretary was Phillip Booker. The interview went like this;

"Good morning," I said, "I've come to apply for the driving job," Names had been exchanged but no handshakes.

Jack Stamp said, "Can you work?

Phillip Booker said, "Yes can you work?"

I said, "Yes I've worked on the farm carrying corn, and mucking out crew yards etc."

Jack Stamp said, "Well you can start in the morning at 8am. The job is more labouring than driving. Bring your driving licence."

And that was it. Another classic interview. Back then, there wasn't such a thing as a CV or Health & Safety, just common sense. The men used to wear flat caps and old jackets, cord trousers, and hob nail boots with steel toe caps. No high vis or hard hats, and company issue stuff either!

My first job was labouring with a bricklayer called Cliff Goodson, nice bloke but scared to death of the boss. We weren't allowed lunch breaks, but still had them, keeping an eye open for the boss turning up to catch us. If he did happen to see you having a cup of tea and a sandwich, he would say,

"Come on Dove it's not a bloody tea party!"

But I used to finish mine before I started work again. I've seen Cliff throw half a cup of tea away and drop a sandwich down the wall cavity just so old Stamp didn't see him.

The lorry I drove was a 1946 Austin three tonner. It had a petrol engine with a crash gear box and it wasn't a tipper!

My first run out with it was to Caistor Sand Pit for a load of building sand; this was a big deal for me driving a lorry all the way to Caistor. The load had to be delivered back to the yard for stock, and I had to shovel it off myself (seven tonne no tipper) but I was young and it didn't bother me. All the tradesmen there were great to work with; we always had a good laugh about some of the things we got up to.

Charlie Barley the painter guy was very interesting, I used to like working with him. He would talk about the 'paranormal' and have you hanging onto every word he said. He claimed he had seen ghosts and spirits and always told me this life is just a short visit for us to learn and do as much good as possible. Was he right or wrong? I suppose one day we will find out. He was a man who would help anyone and loved a joke.

We also had five joiners, two plumbers, five bricklayers, four labourers, then me and Purse Turner, the head lorry driver, (nice bloke).

As the weeks went on I was really enjoying this job, and getting to know all the workmen, as it was my job to take the men to the building sites around the local area. I had a shed type hut on the back of my lorry which was roped down to keep it stable, and then the men would climb on the back of the lorry, and sit in the hut which had two planks for seats down each side and no seat belts either, not much comfort and nobody complained because that's how it was then. And no one ever got hurt.

When we arrived back at the yard at night, old man Stamp would be there with his pocket watch out in hand checking us in. If we were a little early, he would accuse me of speeding and tell me off!

Whilst working at Stamps my social life was very good too. I have already told you about Pam, well then there was Pam Johnson, a lovely tall girl but it didn't last. But I suppose any girl following Pam Clayton had to be special. Jean Sherwood, was also from Goxhill, very pretty and good to be with. Another girl I met was Valerie Shaw who I had danced with at the Drill Hall. She was tall, and had long blonde hair. She came from Brigg, and wanted me to go steady with her, but she wasn't for me.

Then one Saturday night I met Jean Dixon. She came from Barrow, and was a nice girl. It had been this night that I was sat chatting with some girls when a lad walked in the Drill Hall with a girl called Maureen Barton, his name was Frank Watson. He was a cool dude with a pair of shoes on with white tops, drain pipe trousers shirt and red tie. Anyway, later we got chatting upstairs in the coffee bar, and became friends. We still are. Frank was carefree and up for a laugh. He was a Docker at Immingham, and had an Austin A40 car. This was a nice car at that time and he would lend it to me anytime he was at the dance or in Barton.

Whilst I was never into fighting, Frank was always scrapping with somebody. Frank never involved me with any of his confrontations; he always took care of things on his own. It's strange that trouble follows some people, and not others, but I have to say he never went looking for any trouble, he was always happy having a laugh and acting the clown. Frank has always been in my life, and even today Frank and Maureen are in the same darts and domino team as me.

I learned a great deal working at Stamps with all the characters and jobs we did. I laughed all the time working with these lads.

One particular job I remember was sweeping a chimney from the roof down. This is because you couldn't get the cleaning rods up from the bottom. So, George, one of the bricklayers and I were given the job. The house was on Caistor Road, Barton at a very 'upmarket' property. We arrived to be greeted with a snooty middle age lady. Now she knew George and greeted him like this; "Good morning George I am so pleased they have sent you, and not any of the other idiots your company employs."

George in his abrupt manner said, "Any fool can sweep a chimney." I stood back taking all this in and trying not to laugh. George said, "Come on Merv, let's get them ladders off and get on with it then."

It was quite high up to the ridge; our double extender ladder was fully stretched with a crawler ladder on the roof. George had this up in double quick time along with the sweeping rods with a brush on the end. I had to foot the ladders, (that's the only safety we had). George had already been told by the lady which chimney required sweeping. So, there he was stood on the ridge feeding the rods with brush on end down the said chimney, when suddenly out runs the woman covered in soot shouting;

"You blithering idiot you're in the wrong chimney!"

George was a very temperamental sort and chose to ignore her, muttering "I'll give you blithering idiot," and goes faster pumping the brush up and down like a piston! What a laugh. It is a story I will always remember.

Another job with George was building a house at Barnetby. We had a hoist that took barrow loads of bricks up to the top scaffold. It was nearly lunch break and George spotted this barrow arrive up on the top, so he shouted, "Barrow coming down," and kicked it off spilling bricks everywhere, we had to run quick I can tell you.

That's what he was like - crackers! Once, George and I were told to go and unblock a sewerage drain at a posh house up Westfield Road, Barton. This lady never even offered a cup of tea, which upset my friend from the start. After the greeting of; "I'm fed up with this disgusting drain, please hurry and get it flowing again, I'm going out for the day!" she returned to the house. George was saying; "Stuck up woman."

Anyway, we got started and put the rods down the drain, and eventually it cleared and ran free, but I have to say the smell and what was down there was awful. George was well fed up not having had a cuppa, and called her everything he could lay his tongue to as we were packing up.

When she came out and said; "Did you find the problem George? I'm so fed up and disgusted with it!"

"Yeah," he said; "What you have here is a six-inch arsehole going into a four-inch drain Mrs! Come on Merv let's get off."

Well we left her shouting.

"You terrible terrible man, I will ring your boss and report you!

George replied, "Good day Mrs."

It was whilst working at Stamps that I met Marina. Jim, a mate of mine and I went to the dance one Saturday night. We were stood on the side of the hall weighing up the girls when I saw her, small, slim, just over five feet and with long black hair.

I said to Jim, "Not seen her before have you?"

"No," he said, "I think I will ask her to dance."

"No, you won't, I will," I said.

She was quite shy and we had a dance, and then went for a coffee and a chat. I saw her for the next two or three weeks, then one night we were dancing when my mate came up to me and said Pam wanted to see me. So, I excused myself from Marina and went back to Pam for a few weeks, but it wasn't to be and we finished it, and I have to say I was upset.

No More a Bachelor

I would have to wait until August later that year before I saw Marina again. I was at the Drill Hall dance with my mates when she came in with a lad called Pete Sommerscales. She saw me and gave me a smile. I asked her how things were going and she said, "Now you're here good!" It was her birthday, she was seventeen that day.

I said, "What about the bloke you are with?"

She said, "I don't really want to be with him."

So, we had a few dances until she thought it was best to go back to Pete, and no following arrangements were made to meet up.

At that time in my life I had an account with Burton Tailors in Hull. The suits back then were Italian style with drain pipe trousers, white socks, gun metal winkle picker shoes, white shirt and of course the red tie.

So once a month on a Saturday afternoon I would go to Hull. I would take the train from Barton to New Holland then Ferry across to Hull (4 shillings return = 20p now). Going across on the ferry you could sit and have a coffee or a beer if you wanted, there were three ferries back then but the Lincoln Castle was the best one. Looking back now those days seemed so laid back and exciting at the same time, but perhaps it was because we were young and carefree.

Anyway, on this day in September it was lovely and warm when I went to Hull to pay my Burtons account, river like a mill pond and on the way back I'm on the deck just stood looking at the people coming onto the ferry just to see if any of my mates had been in Hull. To my surprise there was Marina and her Mam walking across the deck to the tea saloon. I walked over and said hello, she then smiled and introduced her mother. That's when I first saw Mari (as she was known). We all went for a cup of tea and had a chat. I asked her if she was going to the dance but she said there wasn't a bus on so couldn't come. I told her I would pick her up outside the phone box at East Halton.

Frank loaned me his car as always. We had a great night and got on straight away. She was a good dancer too and we clicked doing the jive. The first time I asked her to go steady was that very night, but she turned me down. However, she did change her mind and we started dating. We got it bad with one another and couldn't wait for the weekends to come around, we even started writing love letters in the week. My good friend Alan Stamp would come around to our house in the week, and we would both sit in our dining room and write love letters. Alan was very good at putting poetry together, and he would write some for me to send to Marina. I have to say at this stage, years later, one day at Orkney Place I went upstairs to find her ripping all these love letters up and destroying them, which I thought was very odd.

At the time Marina and I started dating, Ben got married to Pearl Farmery, and she lived at Goxhill so that's where the wedding was. I was best man for Ben and Marina was also invited. A guy called Len Barley was there with his wife. Len had just bought a new Ford Prefect car, it was a little blue car that you had to start with a handle. Len asked me to take it back to Barton for him that night, and that was to be significant in my travel to see Marina. Len worked for the local baker Birkets in the market place, and always came back at night about 6.15pm. I arranged with Len if I could borrow his car on a Wednesday night. I would be waiting for him to arrive back to the shop and I used to give him ten shillings to have the car for the night. Then off to see Marina where she was living with Beaty in a flat near the Five Ways Grimsby.

Beaty was a lovely Lancashire lady, very funny and witty. When I turned up she looked me up and down and said, "Well you look better than the other one! Hope you haven't got a motorbike like the other idiot."

I said laughing, "No because the crash helmet would mess my hair up!"

Beaty said "Oh God help us," and we had a good laugh.

Borrowing Len's car went on for about nine months and let me tell you, it didn't have a heater, so through the winter months ice would be inside on the windscreen.

This little memory with Len's car was about July. I had collected the car as usual, a little earlier and it was 5.30pm when I started out to pick Marina up for the weekend. Pam had started working at a Grocers in Barton, and used to bike to and from work. This was the first night I had seen her biking home. I stopped to offer her a lift and she sat in the back because I had her bike over the front seat. I dropped her off at Goxhill village end, and yes gave her a kiss. What is spooky; was that very day she had been round to our house to see Gran to ask after me, and ask if I was still with Marina! She even asked me that night if I was happy, and she would like to try again now that she had started work if I was okay with it. I said I was settled with Marina.

Some of the songs we both loved together were; The Shirelles, Will You Love Me Tomorrow, Jonny Tillotson, Princess Princess (the flip side of Poetry in Motion) Everly Brothers Walk Right Back, Eddie Cochran, Come on Everybody, (he was brill) and there were a few more of course.

I think about it sometimes, but the best thing of all was that I got my two lovely daughters which I wouldn't have had if that night I had changed my mind.

I picked Marina up, and this very day she had bought a new white short coat which she had on. When we arrived back at Barton we parked the car and started walking up to our house. It was then I saw an oily black mark all the way down her back on this new white coat. I had to tell her that Len had been careless by putting the starting handle on the seat where she had been sat. Of course, the oil had come from Pam's bike chain, but could I have told her that? I don't think so.

When we got home good old Gran put Fairy Liquid on it, put it in the washer and all was well, well almost but Marina was never happy with it after that and I am not proud of doing that either.

I was still working at Stamps driving the lorry and general labouring, when I saw a little van in the show room at Norman Cox Motors. He had a service garage on Ferriby Road Barton, near the corner with a show room on the opposite side of the road, now a filling station, and hand car wash.

The van was an ex post office series 'E' painted Lincoln green with black wings. The price was £55 no VAT back then, and it was a 1949 model registration number LYK 593. This was to be my first motor. I kept going back to look at it through the showroom window. The year now was 1961 in September and it was common then to see vehicles like this one in show rooms.

I got my heart set on that little van. I was only nineteen years old and couldn't get H.P on my own until I was twenty-one. So, I went to see Ralph asking him to be a Guarantor for me.

I paid a deposit of £10 which was quite a lot for me but I did have it, leaving £45 to pay over 24 months at £2 per month, yes, all Mr Cox charged was £3 for the loan.

Well the day came when I collected my treasured van, it was Friday tea-time and I tell you I was excited to say the least. Paperwork done and then I took it round to show Gran and Pop. They were so pleased for me, and of course Pop says, "Keep them payments up boy and look after it!"

My first run out was to be East Halton. Marina used to come home Fridays for the weekend having stayed in Grimsby with Beaty. At that time, she was working as a machinist at a hosiery factory making ladies underwear, so it was best for her to stay in town all week. When I arrived, I was so excited to show her my little van, I remember taking her for a ride around the block as we called it and she loved it. Marie, and Roy who was Marina's Step-Dad were there to view it too, they both thought it was a good little runner.

To lock the van up I had a metal T shape key that weighed about ½ lb and was 4" long. Starting it was by a switch on the dashboard, then you pressed a button with your left foot to start the engine. The lighting system was six volts against the regular twelve volts of today. It was common to start it with the handle; the gear box was not fully synch so you had to double the clutch (Something people don't know about today). In the back was a proper double seat which could also be laid down and was good enough to sleep on if need be. There was also a large light which illuminated the whole back.

It had been well serviced and looked after. The engine ran on regular petrol (2 star). It was also common back then for small vehicles to run on 'regular' as we called it. The cost of regular per gallon was four shillings = 20p, so five gallons for a quid, (value or what) but it's all relative I suppose. Everything seemed better back then, laidback, and no speed cameras, no CCTV, (which is a good thing for today I know!)

We went miles in that little van and it was also economical, but in the winter months it was a bit chilly because it didn't have a heater, only the deluxe cars (as we called them) had heaters. But I can't recall being that cold. When you're young you don't feel the cold, and I had just met the girl I was going to spend the rest of my life with!

Marina and I would write love letters in the week as well my as visit to her on Wednesday nights. I would then go and pick her up on Friday night to stay with us for the weekend, taking her back on Sunday night. (I have always done the miles for her!)

Christmas came and went and the New Year brought some fresh men at Stamps, one of them was Don Pratt, he was a plumber. Then there was Tom Hardcastle, he was a bricky and a good bloke. Tom was married to Margaret and had three kids. Working with Tom was a good laugh. Marina and I would babysit for them, and Margaret would leave us a fantastic supper of mixed sandwiches small cakes, china crockery all on a lovely dinner trolley. We also got paid ten bob (50p) which was very good back then. Tom and Margaret will be in their early eighties now. How time does fly.

We sat for Don and his wife too, but the supper was not the same as the Hardcastles. I have to tell you this little story about Don's dog, this dog was a powerful bulldog and Don asked me to feed and look after him while they were away on holiday for a week. First night he nearly pulled me off my feet while walking him, so the following night I took my bike around, got him on the lead and off we went. Well! Did we go! He pulled me round the whole estate which was a long way, two miles plus. We came back and he wasn't even panting, he was amazing and so loving, I loved looking after him, and he always made a fuss when I saw him because Don didn't bother much with him. (His name was Tyson).

Autumn was on the way and Marina and I were getting on well, at that time Beaty had retired and moved into a smaller house. This meant Marina had to find new lodgings. This was to be with Jesse and Joyce, and they lived on Balmoral Road opposite the Crow's Nest pub in Cleethorpes. A lovely couple who I got on well with, Joyce worked at the hosiery factory with Marina, whilst Jesse worked for Chambers, a well-known baker and high-class cafe in Grimsby. He drove the delivery van, taking out bread and cakes. He also had a great sense of humour, so we always had a good laugh. I also remember Joyce saying, "Be firm with her Mervin or she will always boss you!"

Back then when you love somebody, you're deaf to those kind of words, but scary stuff when you remember Beaty also warned me too.

Anyway, I was still travelling to and from Grimsby to see Marina and pick her up for weekends, and I have to say having no heater in the van it was cold with proper frosts, and ice on the inside of the screen. I have yet to drive a vehicle or own one with a heater in it. The winters were more severe than they are now, that sounds silly but it is a fact.

The months rolled on, Summer 1962 was lovely, and we had decided to get engaged on my birthday which was the 21st of November. So off we went one Saturday afternoon to Hull, (via the ferry of course). We went to Paragon Jewellers for a look at rings, and Marina saw a Solitaire Diamond Ring which she liked very much, so in we went and I bought it.

Egg & Chips after Midnight

In October 1962, I was on the lookout for a job which paid more money. I had noticed tile lorries in Barton and two of them were owned by a guy called John Usher. I was still working at Stamps as a lorry driver and putting up with verbal grief from the boss. I started thinking more about long distance lorry driving for a living, because I had been told that the tile lorries went all over the country, and I really fancied doing that.

Dark nights came and we were looking forward to my 21st birthday and engagement. I went to see John Usher about a job lorry driving, reason being is because back then, when you reached twenty-one you could drive lorries which weighed over three tons unladen.

John invited me to go with him one night to tip a load of sand he had picked up at Lincoln which had to be tipped at Goxhill Tile Yard in a large shed. If it was left on the truck all night it would freeze and be no good. The Winter was on the way and nights were frosty. I was very impressed going with him sat there in his TK Bedford. The TK had just recently come out and was a lovely truck compared with the heap of junk I was driving at Stamps.

As it was dark nights the green indicator light would go on in the cab, also the control panel had a light too. All this looked so good compared to my old truck which didn't even have indicators. You could hardly hear the engine as it was behind the cab, which gave you plenty of room in the cab with a sleeping bunk. It also had a two-speed back axel giving you eight forward gears (unbelievable back then).

The wages were on a tonnage system, so the more loads you got out and loads of sand back to Goxhill the more you earned. It was possible to double my wages, John was telling me, so to earn over £20 per week was amazing.

My birthday came and also the engagement and we were both excited about the future, and me changing jobs in the New Year. Through the Autumn and dark nights, we kept going to the Drill Hall dances on a Saturday night which we always enjoyed. We usually met up with Frank and Sue, Maureen his old flame had gone and Sue replaced her, but that's another story.

Christmas came with the New Year and a severe Winter to follow, the roads were blocked with snow and hard frost at night. I remember a company in Barton called Screetons who had their own lorries delivering sand to the local building trade. The sand came from their own sand quarry at Messingham near

Scunthorpe. Well this Winter froze up their sand graders and machinery at the quarry.

At Stamps, a lad called Trevor Smith (Smudge) and I were told to go to the sand quarry with some jackhammer equipment to see if we could free the frosted-up machinery! It was an impossible task. Building had come to a halt anyway so no builder was using sand. Trev and I would spend the best part of the day in the work shop, and stand near the big heater and tell jokes with the fitters.

The Winter gradually disappeared and Spring was on the way. The day came when I would give my notice in at Stamps. In those days, you just told the boss you wished to leave the company, no written notices were required, so Monday morning came and I handed in my time sheet and told Jack Stamp I was leaving. He looked up at me from his desk and said;

"What? You can't leave Dove you're wanted here!"

However, Saturday came and I left without a thank you or good luck, just a sour look from him.

My first day out at John Ushers was with a guy called Mike Quickfall, who was John's brother in law and a bricklayer who had been laid off through the severe winter. So, John had offered him a driving job. The lorry I would be driving was the one Mike had until the new one came for him. So, my first run out with Mike was to Scarborough, a full load of tiles to a building site, then sand back from Lincoln. Remember back in those days a trip to Scarborough was four hours at least, so we had to depart Barton at 4am so we could get back in time to load up for the following day. I have to say it was a bit of a shock to my sleeping habits.

Having loaded up that same afternoon for Scotland, I said to Mick "What time will we be leaving in the morning for this one?" Mick said "What? We will be leaving tonight at 7.30pm."

I got to bed for three hours. Poor old Gran said, "You need more sleep than this Merv."

I reassured her saying I could sleep in the truck's bunk. But to my surprise I didn't feel that tired, it was exciting for me to experience turning at Scotch Corner on the A66 heading up Bow Moors Cumbria for our first stop at Sawyers all night cafe situated on the main road A66 in Brough. Mick was good company to be with, the conversation was easy and funny, sharing a few jokes and talking about Stamps where I had just left.

Anyway, gone midnight there we are eating egg and chips and they tasted fantastic. The cafe inside was typical of its day with utility chairs and tables covered with chequered plastic table cloths, and of course the old transport cafe smells of fried food, cigarette smoke, tea and coffee. Drivers sat at the tables consuming large helpings of food and exchanging trucking stories. The cafe, as I learned later in my driving days was always busy, as the A66 is one of the main routes to Carlisle for Scotland.

Having travelled to our destination, Symington near Kilmarnock, we managed to catch three hours of sleep, then the sound of the builders arriving woke us up, we offloaded for 9am then headed back to Lincoln stopping for a hearty breakfast just down the road at a cafe called the 'Tam O Shanto' at New Cumnock.

We arrived at Lincoln sand pit 3.30pm (me driving a lot of the way back). The feeling of being in control of a much larger lorry after what I was used to was amazing. But looking back to those lorries, they were small, compared with lorries of today.

Anyway, in my first week, Wednesday night came and yes, I was ready for an early night in bed. Of course, Pop wanted to know all about my Scottish visit, and Gran was fussing over me with a good meal and fresh clothes after a bath she had run for me, (she was special).

Thursday came and Mick had arranged to pick me up at 6am to take the sand into Goxhill and load up for Skegness and Lincoln, so this was an easy day for us.

Back with sand into Goxhill, load up for Manchester area, Mick said it would have to be a 4am. start. For these "small" runs as we called them, we would always take a pack-up and a flask of tea as we didn't have time to spend in cafes.

Thursday night and we were back at Goxhill with another load of sand and loaded up the last load of tiles of the week for Friday delivery at Great Yarmouth, we also departed at 4am for an 8.30am delivery then across to Lincoln for sand and back to

Goxhill. We loaded up this time for my first solo delivery.

That was a typical week delivering tiles for John Usher doing two to three thousand miles and earning £25 per week average.

I was now looking forward to seeing Marina, as I didn't have time to go in the week. I went through to pick her up to bring her back to our house for the weekend and Drill Hall dance. I still had my little green van and Marina wanted to learn to drive, well this was to be a challenge, to be fair on Marina changing gear wasn't easy for her, as it had a gear box that required doubling the clutch pedal to get a clean gear change. Another thing was that you had to use the side mirrors, as there wasn't a rear view one. So, coupled with these two issues and Marina's short fuse I had to be very patient.

This particular weekend we drove to Kirmington redundant air strip. (Of course, now it's the International Airport). She did okay but decided to go with a driving school later on.

At this time, the songs that were in were The Mersey Sound such as The Beatles, The Searchers, Jerry and the Pacemakers, then there were the American's Roy Orbison, Jim Reeves, The Everly Brothers were still big, Elvis, The Drifters, and many more.

I had loaded up for Scotland again (on my own this time), so I had to leave at 7.30pm Sunday night. Marina by now had left her Grimsby lodgings and moved in with us for a while; she was now working at a hosiery factory called Corah's in Scunthorpe and still making ladies underwear as she did in Grimsby.

It was common to do two Scottish deliveries along with a Shoreham near Brighton and a short delivery in the middle of them. I have to say I loved going to all the different towns and cities. When we delivered anywhere south of the country, we would call at Leighton Buzzard to collect sand for Goxhill. The two sand pits were Arnold's and Garside's; this was special sand for coating the tiles. Now Arnold's are gone and on the land where the company was are private houses, but Garside's are still there trading as they always have. Garside's had their own weighbridge but Arnold's didn't have one, so what we had to do after loading was call at Bedford Cattle Market to weigh at the public one.

Operating this was a lovely old guy, (can't remember his name) but we would give him ten Woodbine Cigarettes, and in return he would put us an extra ton on the ticket. (Remember we were payed tonnage) so this was worth another quid or so.

I can remember the smell of the invoices and tiles and even the cab of my truck, writing my story brings it all back. John Usher who I worked for, had a new Vauxhall Velox, and I have to say he was very easy going and generous.

Pop Taylor had a sister, Edith who lived down in Peterborough with her husband Bill. So, one Sunday Marina and I took Gran and Pop down to Peterborough to see Auntie Ede and Uncle Bill. They were so pleased to see us and surprised, remember not many people were on the phone back then, so they didn't know. They were lovely people, very welcoming and kind. Uncle Bill was a retired engine driver and had forty plus years working on the Great South-Western railway. He told me a story about when he was learning the job. He was the stoker/fireman; this was a hot job keeping the fire topped up for the large boiler which made the steam. It was a golden rule not to stoke up the fire before you entered a long tunnel, because this meant more smoke which hadn't anywhere to go in the tunnel, so you came out the other side black and coughing. Well Uncle Bill got that carried away he didn't spot the tunnel coming up and it was too late to be told by the driver! (But it didn't happen again).

He loved to talk about his engine driving days, and when they visited us at Barrow Mere back when Pearl and I were small, he always gave us 2/6d, they called it half-a-crown = 25p which was a lot of money.

When I was delivering down south and had the time, I would call in to see them and Auntie Ede would fuss around me with beans on toast or fried egg sandwiches with a large mug of tea and one of her homemade scones with thick butter, while Uncle Bill would tell me engine stories.

Uncle Bill died in 1964 of cancer, and Auntie Ede died in 1970. I remember Marina, Ben and I went to the funeral. She was a large lady and I remember thinking it was largest coffin I had ever seen, but bless her she had a heart to match her size; she was just a lovely lady. Auntie Ede and Uncle Bill had one daughter called Ruth, she lives in America and last time we saw her was at her Mother's funeral, but I do remember she was also a very nice lady and promised to keep in touch, but it never happened. If she is alive she must be in her late eighties at least.

An Exciting Engagement

It was 1963, Marina and I were getting on well and couldn't wait to see each other. We had been enjoying our little van for several months when we saw a Morris Minor for sale, so we went for a closer look and I decided to buy it, HP of course. As far as I can remember the cost was £120, registration number MVR 135. It seems crazy but I can remember all my old car registration numbers except the recent ones. Anyway, it was a good little car, four doors, but no heater yet, no radio, but it had a little more comfort than the van.

It was around this time when the sad news came through of the death of Eddie Cochran who was travelling the country with Gene Vincent doing concerts when their car was involved in an accident near Bristol. Oddly, the last record release for Eddie Cochran was Three Steps to Heaven, which was a top chart hit. He was fantastic. My favourite one by him is, Teenage Heaven, it's a good dance song.

So, the Morris Minor we had just got was a 1953 model, colour bottle green, and our first run out was to Scunthorpe to meet up with Mick who I worked with and his wife Pat. They were in the pub called The Cocked Hat, a new pub with a juke box. This was the place to be back then in the Scunthorpe area, you could have a dance to the juke box songs of that time. But I have say back in the sixties the pubs then didn't do food, all that was available was crisps, pickled eggs, pickled onions, and the crisps were plain, cheese & onion, salt & vinegar. There were some pubs that were well supported at weekends that would put on sandwiches; these were the pubs that had a singer on or comic.

Still with our "Moggy Minor," I remember one Saturday morning taking Gran down to Barton Market Place for her to do some shopping. As she got out of the back of the Morris, I said, "leave the door Gran I'll shut it," but she didn't hear me and trapped my finger in the door. Poor Gran she was so upset because she had hurt me. I reassured her that I was fine. But it did hurt and I ended up having it lanced to release the pressure.

Another run out with our little "Moggy," was to visit Kath who lived on the Nunsthorpe Estate with her then husband, Barry Locke, I remember they had two small children Sharon and Kevin. She also made apologies for not having matching glasses as she gave us cold drinks with it being a warm night. This was still 1963 and all those years ago little did I know I would one day be married to her. I remember thinking what a stunningly pretty girl she was and she made us very welcome as she always still does. Isn't life strange sometimes?

I was still at John Ushers delivering roofing tiles all over the country. Then one day I'm on my way to South Wales delivering to Tenby. We delivered to South Wales quite regularly, back then the route down there was A46 all the way to Gloucester going through the towns and cities.

After Gloucester, A38 onto Chepstow, then about ten miles out of Gloucester is Lydney and entering the town is a very steep hill. This is about a mile long and by the time you reach the bottom, the brakes on the lorry are always hot. Well this particular day I had noticed there was a little more travel on the brake pedal than normal and was pleased to reach the bottom of the hill when the red brake light came on telling me the air pressure was low. Luckily for me there was a large truck repair garage in the town so I called in. I soon found out the brakes required some work doing on them. Back in those days the boss would wire money through to the post office so we could pay for the job. In this case I wanted £36. The breakdown delayed me by one day and not wanting my Gran to worry, I phoned my boss' wife so she could let Gran know. I transferred the charges but she wouldn't accept the call. At this point in my life I was getting fed up with chasing about the country delivering tiles, and this incident at Lydney made my mind up to call it a day when I got back.

My delivery that time was to a private house that was having a new roof. They were a young couple with a little girl, and were very kind and let me have a wash, also giving me egg and chips with bread and butter and tea. The little girl now must be in her late fifties. Goodness doesn't time go?

It must have been 6.30pm when I started heading for home en route to Leighton Buzzard to collect sand. From Wales to the sand pit took me through Oxford.

So, I completed the Welsh run and arrived back in Barton telling him to stick his lorry where the sun don't shine!

Mick Quickfall had already left, and had been replaced with an old work mate Ray Hewitt. Ray was the first chap I worked with at Leanings. I liked him, always had a good laugh about day-to-day things. His sense of humour was spot on.

I had gotten to know many drivers who worked for Barrick's, Stamps, and other companies. Barrick's had a guy called Cliff Backhouse driving for them, a colourful character who lived at East Halton.

Cliff died suddenly one New Year's Eve in the Black Bull bar at East Halton a few years ago. I often think about him, and the laughs we had. He would do anything for you, heart of gold indeed.

Then there was Billy Peck, a great guy and always had a joke for you, he had permanent smile on his face. Marina and I would babysit for him and his wife Ann, they lived in a little cottage in Chapel Lane, and for their night out they would go to New Holland club.

They would get back in about eleven o' clock, and he would tell us jokes and have a good laugh, his wife Ann was lovely too.

There were of course many more drivers I worked with, but the ones I have mentioned stand out for me. Billy and Ann have also passed on now. Yes, tile delivery was hard work in those days, in all weathers without pallets and fork lift trucks, but it was accepted as the norm, and I enjoyed it while I was there.

March 1964 and there was me without a job, but as I have said before work was plentiful and we were spoilt for choice. Marina and I had talked about getting married the following year.

At this stage, let me introduce George the hairdresser, he was a Greek Cypriot and a fantastic stylist. His little shop was across from the Wheatsheaf and later in Fleetgate; all us young lads would go there for our Everly Brother hairstyles or any other singing star that was your hero. I stayed with George for years after I left Barton even, travelling from Immingham to have my hair cut properly. I tried others but there wasn't anyone who could come close to George. He had an amazing memory for people's names, every customer old and new would get called by their name. George had moved into Barton in 1963 with his Scottish wife and three children, and soon became a loved character of the town. Sadly, now though we have lost George, and his wife too. Both died in their late sixties of cancer a few years ago.

I was in George's whilst having a haircut when I heard a construction company had set up a large site on Elsham Aerodrome. The company was called CJB (Construction John Brown). This company had won the contract to install a three-foot diameter pipe line to run from North Killingholme to Leicester. So off I went up to Elsham top to see about a job.

A guy called Tom Vickers was the Foreman doing interviews. No appointment as usual back then, just turn up and ask! Tom's nick name was Vick as I soon found out. Having parked my little Morris Minor near the office, coming out a guy said, "You want to be in there mate, they call the guy Vick."

So, I went inside, no fancy receptionist on that site; just a large red-faced chap sat in a chair smiling.

"Nar then mate are ya looking forra job?"

I said, "Yes please, what kind of jobs are they?"

I couldn't believe my ears when he said "What ya like at driving a tractor then?"

Of course, I told him my verbal CV, the wage was £35 (that was brill!) and we had one day off (Sunday).

"How soon can ya start mate?" he said.

The day was Monday, I said Tuesday if that was okay.

"Ye that'll do, we pick up at Wheatsheaf 7.15am, I'd better have ya name then and bring ya P45 and driving licence when ya come in morning. If yav got a minute I'll show the tractor ya going to be driving."

The tractor was a 4 x 4 American Ford Super Six. Brand new I might add, with a cab and duel seat, which was for "Banks Man". In this case, my banks man was a lad called Adrian Smith. Adie was a plump guy but a good worker.

While all this was taking place, Marina and I were talking weddings and looking out for a place to live. My mate Alan was living in a flat in the Market Place with his wife Muriel. The flat was behind Crockett's Dry Cleaners, and was really cosy. Alan told me they would be moving out in the Autumn, and if we were interested he would put a good word in for us. Well we were lucky and got word confirming we had got it. The rent would be £1.2.6p per week = £1.25p, so we were very excited and started saving and collecting a few things. Alan and his wife moved to a little cottage up Barrow Road Barton, and shortly afterwards had a baby boy.

Tuesday morning 7am and I was picked up at the Wheatsheaf along with some more Barton lads, our transport was a large Land Rover with two metal benches in the back to sit on, but it did have a canvas roof. Arriving on site we were given our orders by big Vic as we called him, me on my new tractor with my "banks man" Adie. Our mission was to travel to the redundant air field at Killingholme with a pipe trailer. This was an extension trailer which would carry 3 x 3 and 1.5-ton pipes thirty-six inch in diameter, thirty-five feet in length, so the cargo weighed ten and a half ton.

This was loaded by crane, direct onto the trailer; our job was to deliver the pipes to the pipe line which started at the Killingholme Haven. The tractor was capable of pulling the trailer with pipes loaded through bogs, dykes, or whatever you wanted to throw at it, because the pipe line went as the crow flies, through fields with hedges and dykes. Special bends were made to go under rail lines and roads, and if the tractor got stuck with a loaded trailer, (which was rare) then Adie, my banks man would unhook the trailer. I would then drive the tractor to good ground, Adie would have hitched the winch cable to the trailer, and we would simply winch the trailer clear of the dyke or bog. It was a fantastic tool, impossible to get stuck anywhere. That was Adie's main role, (my lackey!) I mean that in a nice way, he was a good lad.

Well I stayed there driving the tractor delivering pipes until September of the same year. I had earned and saved some money for our marriage for the following year. By now the pipeline had reached Caenby Corner, however the urge had returned for me to get back truck driving.

I had been told by a friend that Barricks of Goxhill required a lorry driver to deliver roofing tiles. Barricks was a good firm to work for, not the mad dash I was on with my first driving job. So, like all the other jobs the interview was unique, but this time I phoned them up as I had got to know them whilst working at my previous tile job. The phone call went something like this;

"Hello is that Alan? (Barrick)"

"Yes," he said.

"It's Merv Dove here I'm enquiring about the driving job."

"Where do you work now Merv?"

Having told him, he said; "So when can you start?"

"Following Monday if that's okay."

"Can you come in Saturday and load up?"

"Yes, okay then."

He told me the wage which was the same as my present job without working Sunday. So, the new driving job was going to help with my savings for our wedding on February 27th, 1965 the following year.

I soon settled in driving for Barrick's and enjoyed the varied work of general haulage and a little more money. With the flat being empty it allowed Marina and I to get on and decorate rooms to our liking. A good friend of mine Graham Ringrose came to do the papering for us. Graham lived in Immingham and completed an apprenticeship to become a professional painter and decorator, he was very good so we were lucky to have his help.

The little flat was taking shape and we were getting excited about living there. A lady called Rae worked in the shop in front of the flat taking in the clothes which required cleaning, from a steady flow of customers. But back then in Barton like all towns of that era, all shops and businesses were busy. Rae was a lovely lady, very friendly and helpful.

Gran had a leather three-piece suite, grey and black in colour and she told us we could have the settee bless her. I remember we went to a furnisher in Barton

called Kenneth Cox, his shop was in Junction Square
where the large card shop is now. We chose a set of
drawers and a side board for the bedroom, along with
a "kitchenette" as they called them, for the
kitchen/living room. This was a cabinet which stored
food etc. in the top half, then it had pull down working
shelf that you could butter bread or cut cake etc. and
then the bottom half had doors where you could store
pots and pans. That was a useful piece of furniture.

Then we bought an electric cooker which went in
the veranda part at the end of the kitchen/living room.
The veranda had a glass roof and we also used it as a
utility room to store shoes etc. I fitted a drop-down
shelf so Marina could work from it when cooking in it
too.

The staircase to the two bedrooms was small and
winding, and we used the bedroom at the rear of the
flat for sleeping. The bathroom (without a toilet)
divided the two bedrooms. The front bedroom
overlooked the Market Place which could be a little
noisy at weekends with people who visited The White
Lion pub next door, so we used this one as a store
room. The toilet was a flush one at the top of the yard
so if it was raining you could get a little wet. For the
evening and through the night we had a potty or 'poe'
for Marina because she didn't like sitting with the
spiders in a draughty loo (Didn't blame her either).

So, there you have a good description of our first
home, and apart from the settee Gran and Pop gave us
we didn't get any help with anything, and of course we

didn't expect any either with Gran and Pop being pensioners in their early seventies. But it just shows that anything you want in life you have to save up for, or get finance on your own to buy it.

I had settled into my new driving job with Barrick's, and Marina and I were still saving up for the big day. Working for Barricks was enjoyable, delivering various cargo all over the country from pig iron in the Midlands to grain for spiller's flour at Newcastle, then roofing tiles down south and Norfolk and always sand back from Lincoln to Goxhill Tiles.

By this time, I had traded the Morris Minor in for a Standard Vanguard Mark 1 registration number FFW 551, a two-tone green car which had some lovely chrome on the front bumpers. The interior had a bench seat with a column gear change. This was quite luxurious and cosy for courting.

Marina had moved from our house, because Gran found it a bit much for her to cope with in a nice way, to next door at Ernie and Doris Milson. This was for a few weeks before she moved to a lady at Scunthorpe in Hempdyke Road called Mrs Martin. She was a lovely old lady, kind, gentle but most of all she was a good cook and looked after Marina and gave her a good breakfast before she did the short walk to Corah's underwear factory.

So, with Marina living in Scunthorpe, I was travelling through to see her on Mondays and Wednesdays and collecting her on Fridays to bring her back home, sometimes to our house or her mother's house at East Halton.

The month was November and Marina had been home for a weekend stay at her mother's when a big row with Roy, who was Mari's husband, in his temper said, "There won't be any wedding here."

Let me tell you a little about Marina's family. Marina's mother, Marianne (Mari) was married to Roy Hopper, who worked at Regent Petrol Company on Immingham docks. He was a steady bloke who was clever at making things like toys and he was good at D.I.Y.

Marina had a step sister called Julie; whose Dad was a bloke out of Grimsby called....... Betts (don't know his first name). But he didn't stay with Mari because he couldn't settle in the country, so he went back to Grimsby.

There was also a little boy called Raymond who was Julie's blood brother with the same father.

Kathleen, to whom I am married now, lived next door to them with her family on a redundant R.A.F camp at East Halton left from the war. These camps were used all over the country because of the housing shortage after the war.

Kath's Dad Jock thought the world of Raymond and bought him sweets and played games with him. Jock had a dog called Bobbie, left behind by the German prisoners. Bobbie would fetch sticks back that kids threw for him.

Well Kath told me a sad story that happened one summer day, she was aged ten at the time. In the corner of the field beyond the camp there was a pond; Raymond apparently was with Bobbie throwing sticks for him when he accidentally fell in the pond and sadly drowned. Mari noticed him missing and went looking for him. She found him face down in the pond, and screaming, she ran back. Some people called Picks had four daughters and one of them ran out on the road to flag down a tanker driver, who waded into the pond and got Raymond out. It was much too late of course and the poor little lad is buried in an unmarked grave in East Halton Church Yard.

Kath and I only a few years ago went to an Open Day at the church and found his death in the church register, Summer 1951 aged three. Kath tells me her Mam and Dad were in pieces over losing him.

The year would be 1959 when they all moved to 7 Abbey View, East Halton. Marina had two Aunties who of course were Mari's sisters, Auntie Evelyn who lived down Cooper Road in Grimsby, and Auntie Pat who lived in Sunderland with Uncle Bob, they were all nice people. On the Hoppers side Roy had a brother called Steve, (a good guy) married with two boys Brian and Trevor who I am still friends with, also he had three sisters Dorothy, Mable, and Rose, I got on well with them all. So that is Marina's family in a nutshell, her welsh side is unknown.

That day of the big row which Marina had with Roy, I picked her up to take her back to Scunthorpe and I could tell things were not good between anyone of them when I entered the house. The 'cheerio's' were said and we left. I have to say Mari was upset with it all and put the blame on Roy, who also had a temper. Had he offered some kind of apology then it could have been different, but that was never forthcoming. Marina kept him to his word anyway, and the wedding took place at St Peters Church, Barton. I could never grab what the row was over anyway.

Still November and I was delivering pig iron to the Midlands, I was now driving a six-wheel Thames Trader, this truck was driven by my good friend Cliff Backhouse who I mentioned earlier in my story. Cliff had left Barrick's and put a good word in for me to drive his truck which was more money for me. We would get loaded in Grimsby and deliver all over Birmingham collecting sand back for Goxhill Tiles, then we would go back to Grimsby all in the same day.

I would leave at 4am and I have to say on a foggy morning with no by-passes or motor ways to the Midlands it was a challenge sometimes. We seemed to have more foggy days back then and frosty mornings to go with them. I was thankful for the heater in Cliff's old truck.

Cliff had gone to drive a road tanker for Pickford's. This job was based at Regent Fuel Oils North Killingholme, the depot was a large underground storage tank farm on the Humber Bank, and all you could see from the surface was very large mounds of grass which was a cover for the storage tanks. The depot had been constructed in 1940 for the war effort and owned by the Ministry. The fuel oil would be delivered into the tanks via ships berthed at the storage jetty.

Pickford's had a fleet of six road tankers delivering fuel oil to Hull and the Midlands. All lorry drivers like myself wanted to be a tanker driver as this was a dream job in those wonderful days.

December arrived and Marina and I had seen a black Ford Anglia car for sale at Birkett's Garage on Barrow Road Barton, so we traded in the Standard Vanguard for it. This one turned out to be a good little car with a great heater, (but still no radio) the registration number TWT 541, so with Christmas on the way and our wedding after in the New Year, we were both getting excited. We had been to see the Vicar; the Rev. W. Sylvester. He was a tall grim figure with a slow stare; he asked if we wanted the word "obey" in the service (this was for Marina to obey)! I know, it didn't work, did it? But to be fair I didn't like that Victorian idea anyway.

On Christmas Eve Marina and I went to the Gaiety in Grimsby with Graham Ringrose who was engaged to Anorah Lee, a pretty little ginger haired girl. It was a good evening but the engagement didn't last for Graham.

My first choice of Best Man was Dave Story, but poor old Dave couldn't do it, at the time he was up and down with depression and a role like Best Man was too big for him. I remember him going in to Lincoln Mental Home once which must have been horrendous for him. When he came home I would take him with me on the lorry, he came with me quite a lot and loved it, always telling people I helped him to recover. I enjoyed his company and didn't realise I was helping him, and for a thank you he bought me some cufflinks which I still have and treasure.

So, Graham stood in and did us the honours.

Married Life

While still working at Barrick's lorry driving, we had got our little flat almost ready for us to move in. Through the winter months I had booked myself into night classes at Bereton School for woodwork, this was so I could make a coffee table, a stool, and a wooden draining board along with a few more bits for us.

January was cold and snowing and travelling at night to see Marina was a challenge but worth it, back then I would be up at 4am to leave for Birmingham with a load of whatever, then load up for the following day, home for tea, cleaned up, changed and out to Scunthorpe to spend time with my future wife talking wedding plans and I can't remember feeling tired.

Of course, I was still at home with Gran and Pop who were very supportive of me. Gran always had good meals ready for me, and all my washing done and Pop wanted to know all my driving stories which he loved. Looking back now I wished I had spent more time with him and talked to him more about his stories of when he was a young man.

I remember fondly one or two that he told me, like when he was First Chap Wagoner and had a team of six horses at Grange Farm Rothwell. He told me, him and another lad would take corn from Rothwell to The Victoria Mills, Victoria Street Grimsby with his six horses and four-wheel wagon loaded with corn. They would leave at 6am travelling on the road out of Rothwell up the hills to Caistor Top and then onto Grimsby, the first large hill going past the pair of cottages on the left was known as 'Boggle Hill.' Pop said this used to make the horses fart as they pulled the large load of corn up the hill. He also used to carry a large heavy stick near his seat, because sometimes the tramps would try to steal his packed lunch that would be stored in a safe box on the side of the wagon along with his bottle of cold tea. He said now and again he would catch one and give them a sore head, telling me he never lost his lunch like some of the others did.

Another story he told me was when Pop and Gran lived at Ferriby Sluice in 1934, Ralph used to take Ben to school on his crossbar. The farm they were on was owned by Farrow's of Wootton and with the land being clay type soil it was very heavy and most of it was ploughed with two big traction engines which stood at each end of the field. The large plough was dragged across the field with cables under slung below the steam tractors; he says it was a spectacle to watch and 'high tech' in those days. Back then he told me, he usually stayed at a farm for one year then moved on to better himself. (Or so they hoped).

January 1965 and by now The Beatles were getting very big in the music world along with the other

'Mersey Sound' music. We weren't keen and were still locked in with Everly Bros, Elvis, Cliff Richard, Ricky Nelson and all the rest of the fabulous early sixties singers. The country and western music was getting big though and we also liked that. We were beginning to hear about Jim Reeves, Jonny Cash, Patsy Cline, Marty Robbins, there were of course many more, yes and Slim Whitman was still big in the country music world.

February arrived and we had decided to have our honeymoon in London. Marina had picked her bridesmaids too, they were to be; Eileen, her friend from Grimsby, her step sister Julie, and my cousin Jane, (Ralph and Marjorie's daughter). Our little flat was all ready and the wedding day was close. We could only afford cake and wine for the reception which was held at the Chapel Recreation Hall down Chapel Lane. We hired Woollies from Barrow who were wedding specialists in the reception field. Ralph and Marjorie had suggested Marina leave from their house for the church, at that time they lived in an end house near the school I attended in Council Terrace. I remember taking her down to their house the night before the wedding and both of us very excited, and then Graham and I went off to have a drink in Waltham at The Kings Head. (Fancy Waltham of all places). In those days though, stag nights weren't that popular and I was back home for eleven o'clock.

The big day came and I went in the morning to get my hair cut at George's, of course him having his little bit of humour saying it wasn't too late to change my mind. Anyway, two o' clock came and there I was sat in the front seat in St Peter's with Graham my best man waiting for Marina to arrive. I had chosen my cousin Terry Teasdale to be my usher who was doing a good job. I remember it was bitterly cold with flakes of snow coming down but they didn't settle thank goodness. Marina arrived with Ben who was giving her away. I remember she looked so pretty and delicate in her wedding dress with her lovely long black hair to compliment it all.

The ceremony went off without a hitch and before we knew it, there we were having our photos taken as Mr and Mrs M. Dove with a very young David Lee. I remember having toothache come on as we stood there, but I just had to keep smiling. I couldn't wait to get back in the warmth to our reception which went down well considering it was only cake and wine.

The only thing was when speech time came and I forgot to say; "on behalf of my wife," which she reminded me of later with her sharp tongue. I apologised, saying I had been nervous and had toothache! It was no excuse, but it was a storm in a teacup and soon forgotten, until our wedding day came up in conversation in the following years, then it was remembered all over again!

That evening about five o' clock we set off for London on our honeymoon and those days remember, the route was through Brigg, Lincoln and onto Newark to pick up the A1. We travelled down to Baldock, where there was an all-night café, restaurant called

Jack's Hill. We went into the restaurant and remember very well that we had chicken and chips with peas, and because Marina had a brand-new ring with confetti still hanging around it, the waitress leaned over as she gave us our meals and said 'congratulations'.

Having had our meal, we left for London in our little Ford Anglia and headed for a small hotel in Victoria. It was getting late so I paid 10s to a taxi driver so we could follow him to the hotel. (Remember 10s. = 50p was a lot of dosh then) We arrived at the hotel about eleven o' clock.

When we got in our room I took off my jacket and put it on the white candlewick bed cover. Well! There were little white bits all over it! Needless to say, Marina told me how stupid I was for doing such a silly thing and I had to agree.

Shattered, we turned in for a good night's sleep, the following morning we were late up and missed breakfast, but who's bothered about that when you're just married?

We stayed in London for four days I think, I remember we went to see the Cleopatra film starring Elizabeth Taylor as it had just been released. Afterwards we went and had tea at a Lyons Corner House which was very popular in the sixties. But I was a very faddy eater and decided to have Gammon, but (wait for this!) somehow, I had got it in my head it was Fish. Marina did say it was Ham but I wouldn't listen and was disappointed when it came. But Marina did say it was the worse piece of Gammon she had ever seen. We started talking about our little flat waiting for us back at Barton, so we cut short our honeymoon and went home.

On arrival, back at our little flat, Arthur, who was married to Mary (Auntie Ethel's daughter) worked nearby at a printers and spotted us arriving back, so he came out with his movie camera and made a little film of us offloading the car and carrying our things in (I think Marina still has it on VHS).

We settled in and both started back at work the following week, Marina at Corah's in Scunthorpe and me driving for Barricks. Marina had to be up every week day at 7am to catch the bus to work, while I was still getting up early hours to make deliveries in the Midlands.

Shortly after I had started back from our honeymoon, I was driving an old-style lorry which was used for local work and my job was to lead pig iron off the Royal Dock in Grimsby to the iron dump in Adam Smith Street. Hartwell Motors stands on the dump now. It was the last load of the day when I was tipping it and the pig iron slipped to one side causing the body to twist, also creating a problem for the tipping rams which wouldn't come back down, so the body was partly tipped. I had no choice but to head for the yard back at Goxhill with the body half tipped up. Going back down Boulevard Avenue, which takes you under the railway subway, the rams hit the large iron bridge and knocked the rams off, this experience is still now quite clear in my mind but Barricks were very good about it and said don't worry about it.

Spring time was on its way and I was getting a little fed up of early mornings. Geoff Herrick, who was married to my cousin Maureen drove for Scunthorpe Hauliers based at Brigg. We saw them out one weekend when he told me there was a job going at his depot, the job was delivering tarmacadam to places like Hull, Selby, and Boston, from Glugstons at Scunthorpe. Getting up at 6.30am instead of 3.30am sounded a much better option. I didn't have an interview, Geoff just put in a good word and I started the following Monday. The money was no better but the job was.

Marina also had a job move and went to work for Cottingham's butchers and bakers in Barton High Street (now long gone).

I started driving for Scunthorpe Hauliers about April time 1965. The truck was a four-wheel TK Bedford, same as the one I had on the tile job. The only downside was that I had to travel to Brigg by car before I could start work, but petrol was still very cheap so cost didn't matter.

The boss and owner was George Read who was a good bloke, sadly he had just lost his wife and often wanted to talk about her. He only had five lorries which were always kept clean and tidy. I had my cab polished up all the time as we had plenty of spare time between loads. From Barricks to this was like a holiday.

Marina was also enjoying her new job, the minced beef pies she sold at the shop were the best I have ever tasted and still are, and when you cut them open the lovely thick gravy just flowed out. We would have these twice a week for our tea with potatoes and vegetables which was wonderful.

Marriage was going well and we settled into a routine. Summer was on the way and we were talking about a holiday. At this time, we were friends with Graham Ringrose's brother Terry, and his very funny wife Ann, she was a good laugh. They lived in Immingham down Bluestone Lane in a lovely detached house that he designed and built himself. Terry was a joiner and worked for a local company called Staintons.

One night when we visited them they told us about Cornwall and how lovely it was, Loo in particular they said was so picturesque. So that did it, Cornwall was to be our first holiday.

Around this time having done a few more coach trips on Mick Smaller's Coaches he asked me if I was interested in taking my PSV test so I could drive for him part time. Of course, I said yes and after a few times with him he thought it was time to put in for my test.

It was 1965, the month was July and my test for the bus was due. I chose to take it in a double decker. This old bus was a crash gear box 1953 Leyland.

Back in my days as tractor driver for Andrews I took my driving test on a tractor. The guy who was the examiner that day was called Mr Wynn and I passed first time. That day the test was for me to drive the tractor up the road and back, reverse around a corner to park up, then a hill start using the hand brake and that was it.

Well the bus road test I took that day was in Scunthorpe and the examiner was our Mr Wynn. The test consisted of me going up and down the gear box which isn't easy with a crash gear box, because you have to double your clutch every time, using a set of traffic lights, reversing around a corner without touching the kerb, and answering a few questions. I thought the whole test was easy and yes, I know I sound boring but I passed that one first time too. So that gave me my PSV Licence No. EE 41603, and I still have it for you to see. The licence badge came from Nottingham, and the EE stands for the area you are from.

August arrived and off we went on our first holiday to Loo in Cornwall, we still had our Ford Anglia 100E and it was going well. Back then it was quite an interesting journey with having no motorways.

We decided to depart at midnight because we couldn't wait and it sounded romantic. It was so exciting for us with it being our first holiday and travelling all that way. I remember we stopped at Stow-on-the-Wold for a hot dog and coffee which folk were selling in the large town centre, they tasted delicious. Also in them days you didn't tend to pre-book, so we were on our way through all the towns and villages, and I remember how lovely it was compared to how travel is today.

For one thing, you didn't have to worry about CCTV or speed cameras everywhere or struggling to park up or massive traffic jams, or yellow lines like there is today.

Having arrived down in Loo that afternoon we parked outside a little hotel in Harbour Street. I remember the sound of the seagulls and the lovely smell of the sea. The hotel overlooked the harbour and the view was so wonderful, we had seen nothing like it. We went into the hotel to ask what rooms were available. Having been shown a double room which we loved, we were pleased to stay there for the week. I don't recall us having our own en-suite and of course there weren't TV's or tea and coffee facilities in the room. That was just the way it was then, unless you wanted to pay high prices, but you still wouldn't have TV, there was only black and white anyway.

The holiday went well with lovely sunshine and good food, the only little hiccup was when Marina wanted her hair doing and we had to find a hairdresser for her, there is a photo somewhere with Marina stood outside the shop and hair looking posh.

The week went quick and we promised ourselves that we would be back, and we did go back but with Malc Hardy and his then wife, Bobbie.

We were still friends with Frank Watson and his wife Sue; they lived at Immingham in a caravan behind the garage at the bottom end of the town. Occasionally we would go to have tea at their place. After tea, they would arrange a babysitter and we would go to the Conservative Club to see a local act performing, they were good nights at the club back then.

Autumn was on the way and this particular Sunday we had decided to stay in for home cooked lunch. Marina was a good cook and I remember her doing a chicken dinner. I popped next door to the White Lion, (which is a card shop now) for a pint and to see the lads, and as promised I was back for one o' clock. We sat down at the little table we had bought to have our dinner on and ended up with the dinner on our knees. I had put leaves up on the collapsible table and hadn't locked the support hinges in place. With it being new it was very stiff and I thought they were fixed. Well Marina wasn't too impressed with me but we did end up having a laugh later, and I learned from the experience to make sure the support locks were in place!

August of that year came and Marina celebrated her 21st birthday but I can't remember what we did for it as you didn't make such a big fuss back then. We had two friends called Les Austin and Carol Keeton, Carol lived in Immingham with her Mam and Dad (really nice folk), Les lived with his Mam and Dad in Goxhill (also nice people). Les and Carol would come over now and again and we would go out or stay in and Les and I would share jokes whilst the girls would have a good chat.

On August Bank Holiday in 1965, we all decided to go to the Derbyshire Dales for the day; Les said his Dad would lend him his new car which was a Triumph Herald and a very nice car of that era. Les said bacon and eggs tasted really nice cooked in the open air so that would be our Bank Holiday lunch and he would do the cooking, so having all contributed to eggs and bacon etc. and Les supplying his Dad's portable cooking stove with frying pan we set off for the Derbyshire Dales.

We were singing to the radio and I remember Manfred Man was on singing his new song "Pretty Flamingo," when suddenly, we came up to a traffic queue just around a corner. Now Les was a steady driver thank goodness and just like slow motion slid into the car in front and nudged it a little with no harm done. The roads were already damp as the weather was turning wet, but if they had been dry we would have stopped quite easily.

Anyway, we carried on looking forward to our fried lunch, and on arriving at the Derbyshire Dales the weather had turned and it was a typical bank holiday absolutely pissing it down. Well this didn't deter Les.

"Come on," he said in a cheerful voice, "Let's get started."

I'm looking at Marina. She looks at me in disbelief, I mean we were well ready for home and it had also turned cold just to add to our misery. So, there was Les with his little gas stove, frying pan on with bacon going and a coat over his head to keep the rain off. By this time the rain was persistent. Us three were sat in the car and Carol was getting fed up like us, when Les shouts;

"First one ready!" Carol collects it from him and gets back in the car. I have to say it did smell good but looked awful, cold runny fried egg, bacon well done on one side and hardly cooked on the other. Marina was whispering to me, "I'm not eating that!" I had to agree I wasn't keen.

Anyway, Carol says; "Les! Let's pack up and go home."

To our relief he agreed. We three thanked him for his positive effort and headed home. (Home was our little flat) Only the day before Marina had cooked a chicken, so that was to be our meal with salad, a mountain of bread and butter, fresh cups of tea and a good warm up. Of course, we had a good laugh then about our "Frying Bank Holiday," and later years too.

Les was a good piano player and singer, and sometimes at his Mam and Dad's we would have an evening singing and I would tell a few jokes. (I'm still telling the same ones now, ha ha) We lost touch with Carol and Les as they too got married and went to live in Goxhill having two children, who of course are now grown up and have children of their own. I have learned only recently that poor Carol is very ill, but good old Les being the sort he is, has took on being her full-time carer. But that memory of the 'fry up' in the Derbyshire Dales is very much still with me, and I have happy thoughts of our friendship with them back then.

It was Saturday morning at Scunthorpe Hauliers, and the boss asked me and Geoff, another driver, if we would load up Sunday morning (double time pay). The load had to be delivered to Bradford railway station car park for 7.30am Monday morning, so on Sunday evening about 9.30pm, Marina and I went to bed as I had to be up at 4.30am. Back then getting out of bed wasn't my favourite thing, so just to be sure I had four alarm clocks. The Baby Ben (which I still have and it works) was tied on the on/off cord for light above my head about four inches from my ear (and I wasn't deaf then). So, all these clocks would go off one at a time. The emergency one was in a biscuit tin on the dresser so I had to get out of bed to stop it.

I have to tell you we slept through all this only to wake up at 7.30am Monday morning, with the sun coming in through the crack in the curtains. "Look how late I am, I should be in Bradford now!"

Marina was okay as she was working at the bakers in Barton. I dressed extra quick and in my little Ford Anglia drove like hell to Brigg, of course Elsham level crossing was closed for two trains just to add to the panic, so I arrived at the yard about 8.10am went all the way to Bradford arriving 10.30am, only to have my load rejected, so I came all the way back to tip it on the reject dump. I have to say; my boss was not best pleased.

The month was October 1965 and I had been to Hull delivering Tarmacadam. On the way back I stopped for a cuppa out of my flask when Cliff drove in behind me. He was working for Pickford's on a fuel oil contract working out of Regent Oils Killingholme. This tanker driver job was one of the best ones to have if you were lucky enough to get a start. Cliff told me he had been looking out for me to talk about a driving job coming up and was I interested in applying?

Of course, I looked at Cliff in disbelief, "Am I interested?"

I explained I was, but that I had no experience in tanker driving, Cliff said, "No problem training will be given, and because I'm recommending you for the job you will get it."

I couldn't wait to get home and tell Marina the good news; she was as excited as me with the thought of a job improvement and a little more money too.

My interview was to be at East Halton to see a guy called Eddie Jones. He was the driver Foreman overseeing the daily activities of the other drivers and posting time sheets to the headquarters at Manchester. My appointment time was after tea that same night after seeing Cliff that day. Cliff told me to just turn up after tea because he would see Eddie at work and tell him to expect me. None of us had phones but still everything fell into place.

This interview was pretty much the same as the others. Having knocked on the door about 7pm, Mrs Jones opened it and asked me in, inviting me to sit down in the front room. Eddie came in smiling, we shook hands and then he started having a laugh about Cliff and me knowing such a character. He asked about my driving knowledge and experience, and of course I told him about my long-distance days on the roofing tile job, then working at Barricks and also passing my PSV test to drive a double decker bus. He told me the wages and hours per week and said I would be driving an eight-wheeler AEC Mammoth Major. I had noticed Eddie had a lovely Irish accent and talked as though the job was mine all the way though the interview.

I was to start work the first week in November if that suited. "Of course," I responded, that meant giving two weeks' notice at Scunthorpe Hauliers which was much better than just one week. We shook hands again and I thanked him, leaving to drive back to Barton. I was so excited and couldn't wait to tell Marina. She was so pleased for me.

The daily deliveries of fuel oil were steady drives out to places like Nottingham, Leicester and Hull. We were given eleven hours per day to make the deliveries and didn't even have to load the tanker because it was done for you by the yard loaders. Compared to the other driving jobs of having to load yourself and chasing about all over the country, this was going to be a breeze.

Whilst all this was happening for me, the local council at Barton had just commenced making Market Lane wider. This was the approach road from Blue

Bell corner up into the Market Square; it was common to see a double decker bus waiting at the top of the lane waiting for clear access before going down the lane. The widening of the lane meant a few shops were going to be demolished, along with a few old houses. This was a sad time for a few of us as Bill Doughty's sweet shop was going to go. Stead & Simpson's shoe shop on the corner of the Market Square was going too. Whilst sad, because I really don't like change, all of this had to happen, because vehicles were beginning to get bigger and there was a little more traffic being noticed too.

I am proud to say our Uncle Ralph was now the general Foreman in charge of many men and projects as well as the Market Lane one. Our Ralph; from general labourer to highways superintendent. This always makes me feel proud of him as well as the fact that he such a good genuine man.

By this time, I was thinking about giving in my notice to leave Scunthorpe Hauliers and thinking about my new tanker driving job. George Reed, my boss, accepted my notice and wished me well.

Our special Gran was still doing our washing for us with Marina doing the ironing. My input was to deliver and collect the washing. I really don't think that until now when I reflect, we appreciated her as much as we should have.

I worked my notice and was looking forward to starting work at Regent Fuel Oils driving for Pickfords.

My first run out was with Eddie the Foreman with a delivery at Nottingham Coop.

Let me take through a typical day as a tanker driver for Pickfords. We were paid from 6am but didn't get to the depot until 7am (this was all okayed by Eddie), then we would have a chat in the mess room and leave the depot at 7.30am (tanker loaded for you). If your delivery was the Midlands then the first job was breakfast at Welton Hill cafe near Lincoln, arriving there about 8.30am. Having had a good chat and laugh with all the lads who used to congregate there and breakfast of course, we would then leave about nine thirty and head off to our delivery (in my case Nottingham). We would arrive at 11.30am, remember back then the route would take you through all the towns and cities making the journey slower but much more interesting as the tankers were flat out at 40mph.

It would normally take one hour to pump off the load, and whilst this was going on you would be sat in the boiler house with the guy in charge having a cup of tea and a joke or two. Having pumped it off, it would then be a steady ride back to Killingholme.

We were allowed one and a half hours for delivery so on the way back it was quite easy to make up some cafe time. We would all meet up back at Welton Hill cafe and I have to say that new driving job was a pleasure. Eddie let me have a drive back and I remember being sat behind the wheel of that large tanker, it was amazing with good views, the big engine throbbing away, the oily smell and I felt like 'King of The Road.' Yes, I was certainly going to enjoy this job.

We arrived back at the depot at 5.15pm, having been allowed eleven hours for the delivery. Compared to any other driving job this one ranked well at the top, and this was all thanks to my good friend Cliff Backhouse who had recommended me for this wonderful opportunity.

Over the next few weeks I settled into my new job like a duck to water, and Marina was still working at Cottingham's bakery which had now become Smith's as old Mr Cottingham had retired. David Smith, who had bought the business, was the son of Cliff Smith who had a long-established butcher's business in the Market Place. I knew David from school, and the whole family were well-respected and liked.

Christmas was close and we had made arrangements with Graham Ringrose and his girlfriend Anorah to go to the Christmas Eve dance at The Gaiety in Grimsby, a young Pat Volley was singing with his band and it was a fantastic night. Dance nights at the Gaiety were always good, the place had an air of romance about it and once again I can't remember any trouble or fights with anyone.

New Year 1966 came and a lot happened in this year. At that point in our lives Marina and I weren't going out so much as we were saving up to move out of the flat. We had been chatting about moving to Immingham to live. Terry and Ann with whom we were friends and visiting at the time told us builders were building some maisonette flats above the shops on the brand-new Kennedy Way shopping centre. This interested us for many reasons, the main one was that it would cut down travelling time to work, and Marina could easily get a job at Byford's Hosiery Factory (a trade she had learned previously).

We made enquiries and received a letter offering us one in the September. It was spring time, so we were getting excited about living in "Tin Town" as they used to call it.

I was still enjoying my tanker driving job, when my friend from Barton, Alan Portess came to work with us. Alan was a real good mate, always ready to help and he had a fantastic sense of humour. He is sadly no longer with us.

One morning I got ready for work and went out to my car to leave at 6.30am. I went to the usual place where I had left it the previous night which was Sunday. After seeing it wasn't there I thought I must have left it in the Market Place, but no it wasn't there either. I quickly concluded that it had been stolen. I reported it missing to the Police then managed to get a lift to work.

I found out from the police on the Wednesday that they had found it on a farm near Elsham Golf Course. Apparently, some youths had stolen it for a ride back to Brigg and left in the farm yard. Alan Portess drove me over to collect it to find the dash broken and ignition hotwired, but apart from that everything was okay. I have to say that theft was rare in those days. I never heard if the lads got brought to book over it, but I was pleased to get my car back in one piece.

It was at this time that I bought a motorbike from Roy Hopper, a BSA 125cc but I didn't get on with it and sold it on. The idea of having one was to save fuel but back then fuel wasn't a big issue anyway.

Summer was on the way and the football World Cup had started, I remember taking Graham Ringrose with me on the Saturday as the final was played at Wembley. Our delivery was at a hosiery factory in Leicester and we were on our way back by lunch time. We made it back to his Mam's house in Immingham for 3.30pm in time to see the second half. I have heard people say; where were you when England beat Germany in the World Cup final? Well that's where I was! It's something you just don't forget. (Especially hammering Germany!)

Lots happened for Marina and I in 1966. One night in late August we paid a visit to Terry and Ann's at Immingham and it was that night they told us about Taylor and Coulbeck, a Cleethorpes building firm building bungalows just off Washdyke Lane Immingham. After making enquiries we learned that a three-bedroom detached bungalow on a decent plot of land was priced at £2,650. This was based on me painting the windows and doors myself and no garage. Mortgages back then weren't easy to get but we did manage one based on an endowment system.

Maple Grove

Our own property was to be 2 Maple Grove, so it was time (with pleasure) to cancel our Immingham flat with the council which wasn't a problem. We were both very excited about owning our own property and couldn't wait to tell Gran and Pop the good news. I could see the proud look on their faces and it was wonderful because we were the first in our family to start paying for our own property.

Marina's Mam and Step-dad were pleased too because paying a mortgage was a little rare in those days, I remember the payment for the mortgage was £13.10s. The endowment payment was £7.17s.6p This coupled together was quite a lot for us to pay. So, there we were all signed up and looking forward to a completion date for our new home.

September arrived and I received word that the contract which Pickford's had with Regent Fuel Oils was to terminate in October, talk about gutted! You wouldn't believe how we both felt, a bit low to say the least, as did all the other drivers. However, as the saying goes; 'When one door closes another one opens,' and it did.

But the best door to open has yet to come.

Caledonian, a tanker company based on Manby Road Immingham and part owned by Pickfords wanted some tanker drivers. Also at that time some of the drivers got started at Shell Petroleum, whilst some others moved to Birmingham to drive tankers for Texaco which replaced Regent. So, a lot was happening in the tanker world in those days.

Along with a few other drivers, Alan Portess and I started work at the beginning of November 1966, and I have to say it was a sharp contrast driving for Caledonian compared to Pickfords.

A guy called Morris Wright was the transport foreman (a nice bloke) who would let you work any hours you liked. The manager on the other hand was full of himself.

In the meantime, we were keeping an eye on the building of our new home. It's a shame we didn't take any photos of the building stages, but people back then didn't use the camera much anyway.

Christmas came and went and it was at this stage our little Ford Anglia was beginning to play up and wouldn't start in the cold January mornings.

It is of course 1967 and I am telling Alan Portess my friend about the bad starting. Alan says it needs a top engine overall.

"Would you like me to do it?" he said.

Of course, I jumped at the chance to get it done, so Alan arranged for our car to go into his brother-in-law's garage where it was a little warmer. The overall went well with Alan being a qualified motor mechanic, (which I didn't know).

While the overall was going on, something tragic happened in my life.

You remember me talking about Alan Stamp, a real good friend of mine who lived in the flat before us. Well the date was close to Gran Taylor's birthday which was the 25th of January. Around the 23rd I learned sadly that Alan had died in an accident. He drove a lorry for a transport company from Barton and it happened whilst travelling from a sand quarry near Doncaster fully loaded en route to Sandtoft Tiles for delivery.

As far as we can understand, Alan had passed some workmen repairing the road, went onto the soft verge and lost control. On each side of this particular road there were deep drains, probably fifteen feet at least with four to five feet of water too. The coroner report said he was knocked out and drowned in about eight inches of water that had seeped into his cab. As well as losing poor Alan, his little dog died with him too. I just couldn't believe that he had gone and that I would never see him again. The funeral was one of the saddest ones to which I have ever been with him only being twenty-eight years old.

After the funeral Dave Story and I went back to our flat for a cup of tea as there wasn't a wake or anything to attend.

Alan is still as fresh in my memory as he was then. With all the laughs we had, the dances we went to and the girls of course, Topp's Cafe at Immingham with frothy coffee and the fabulous Juke Box, the "Tin Mission Hut" Rock n Roll dances and much more with him, who could forget Alan with his old Austin A40 Devon model.

So, Alan Portess did my engine overall for me, and it went like new! Started first time in the cold mornings, went smoother and much better all round. Amazing. Alan wouldn't take anything for doing it and that is a friend.

Whilst all this was going on, my sister Pearl had met a guy called John Latham who lived in Scunthorpe. He was a nice chap, originally from Leicester. Pearl and John married and lived in a flat on Frodingham Road. Marina and I would visit them sometimes and because they cooked, slept, and lived all in the same room there was always a cooked food smell I remember.

March 1967 and we were all ready to move into our bungalow. Terry Ringrose had offered to help us move and I remember Terry bringing a ladder with him on his roof rack so that we could carry the wardrobe down the ladder out of the front bedroom window overlooking Barton Market Place. (Health & Safety at its best!) Then we placed it on the back of a pickup truck I had borrowed along with the other stuff. I remember we had two trips to clear it all and it was so exciting for us sleeping in our new home for the first time with the smell of new paint and a flush toilet in the same property. It was amazing to have that again.

Waking up the first morning in new surroundings was a real pleasure, and I remember it was a lovely spring morning to make it a warm welcome to Immingham.

As we settled in our new home, The Torrey Canyon oil disaster happened off the Cornish coast near Falmouth.

March 18th, and I was still working at Caledonian Oil Tankers when the notice went up in the mess room wanting volunteers to deliver special oil solvent to the disaster. So, I decided to go for one week along with another driver called Brian Horsewood. I remember we left the depot the following Sunday afternoon in two Leyland Octopus tankers. These vehicles were eight wheelers with a top speed of 40mph and were very noisy as well as uncomfortable.

Our first call was to be Pumpherston near Edinburgh to collect our load of detergent from a Shell Refinery. The journey up to Shell is a little faded but I think we arrived Monday afternoon, and by the time we both got loaded it was Tuesday morning. That day we made it down to Carlisle I remember well, because we stayed for the night on London Road in transport digs, what an eye opener! There I saw drivers sleeping fully clothed just laid on the beds which of course were filthy. I was the youngest one and felt a little intimidated by the whole experience of being there. I can't remember breakfast but the next stay over was Bristol, and I remember we had a large square sign on the front grill of the tanker which had a big red TC on it letting everyone know where we were going.

Just to remind you, the only motorway we travelled on was the M6 and there was only thirty miles of that, with no by-pass around Birmingham. As we travelled through the towns and cities the Police would hold up the traffic to allow us priority and this made us feel special with big TC on the front and some people waving at us.

I can't remember what the digs were like at Bristol but I do remember it was a hard slog driving that old tanker, going up and down the gear box all day arriving at Falmouth harbour side Thursday tea-time. Brian, with whom I travelled, was a good friend with much more experience than myself and he certainly looked after me.

I had now been away since Sunday and not been able to speak to Marina to see how she was doing on her own. Can you imagine no mobiles or computers to keep in touch? But that is how it was, and life still went on quite well without all that technology.

So back to Falmouth, the digs were immaculate I remember, but as we sat down with a few other drivers for our evening meal I noticed a couple of drivers had already got their meals. Well I'm looking at the food and thinking 'That looks awful!"

It was minced beef with vegetables and mashed spuds. The mince was pale, the vegetables were watery and the mashed spuds were sloppy. Mine arrived and yes just like the others it was gross! After two forkfuls, I said I was too tired to eat and excused myself.

"Don't tha want it lad?" said one of the drivers in a broad Yorkshire dialect.

"No thanks," I said.

"Well, pass it over ere lad, tha can't waste it can tha!"

At that moment, the very nice and understanding landlady came over and said; "Maybe my treacle sponge would go down better for you love." It did and with the most delicious creamy custard.

I'm thinking now about the drivers there, and sadly they will all be passed on as they were all much older than me.

After breakfast, we were escorted with RAF Personnel a few miles down the road to Helston RAF Field, from where the cleaning up operation was being co-ordinated. We soon learned that the load of detergent we had was to be offloaded into 40-gallon drums (and we both had 4,000 gallons each) so that they could be handled once down on the beach at the disaster area.

So that was Friday morning and by the time Brian and I were offloaded it was about 6.30pm, so the RAF lads offered us digs for the night in their billets which of course we were glad to accept. The bed was comfortable and I had a well-earned sleep followed by the lads shouting, "Breakfast On!"

This is when I had a taste of the Forces life; we were in this large mess room forming a line holding our plates and the staff sergeant shouted, "Keep moving lads hurry up and make up your mind what you want!" Well by the time it got to my turn I was ready as I had had time to view the menu.

Bacon, eggs, beans, fried bread, sausage, three toast and tea (no milk) and I have to tell you it was one of the best fry-ups I have ever had.

Whilst eating all this Brian said, "We are heading for home now Merv, I don't know about you but I've had enough!"

I had already made my mind up I was going home anyway so I said, "Well that suits me Brian."

So, Saturday morning about 9am we headed for home, and what an eventful week it had been. I couldn't wait to see Marina, and wondered how she was and how she had managed on her own. I arrived home about 1am on Sunday morning, tired out but so pleased to be home with Marina again. She too was pleased for my return because she had had no idea when I was coming home.

I could now get settled into sorting out the back garden and putting a path down for the washing line. Now let me tell you where the path came from for our garden. Around the corner in Oaklands Road lived Stuart Ringrose. Stuart had spotted some pavers down Habrough Road that the council had left, these had been used and were perfect for my requirements. So late one night Stuart and I went with his work's van and got twelve of those pavers! (I know it was wrong but they made an excellent path.)

We had a coal bunker near the back door to which we had small coal delivered from Cullum's for our coal fired stove which gave us hot water and heat in the kitchen (No central heating yet). It was about the end of March when we were introduced to Glynn and Connie Driver who had moved into the bungalow opposite us. Glynn was a manager for Fison's Fertilizers which is now Norsk, and Connie worked at Byford's where Marina worked. We became very good friends with them and it was Glynn who introduced me to darts in a big way.

I always liked and had played the game but it was Glynn, a very good player who taught me a lot about the game and saw I was good enough for a team. On Friday nights, we would go to the Bluestone and back in those days darts was a lot bigger in pubs than it is today, so we would put our name on the chalk board for a game and if we lost early it was a struggle to get back on that night because of the volume of people waiting to play. If that happened we used to go to Habrough and play at the Station Hotel.

Marina and Connie became good friends and did quite a lot together. Connie and Glynn had three children; Glynn the son, Glynis, their eldest daughter and Dorothy the youngest. I always liked Dorothy, she was a lovely girl and still is. Glynn (son) has died but Glynis is living in Turkey and Connie and Glynn are sadly deceased too.

The neighbours back then were all nice people and easy to get on with. On the right side were Sylvia and

Len Picking with two boys Richard and Philip, they were only little boys then but will be in their early 50's now. Next to them and at the side of our back garden were Kath and Ted Trigg with two boys from Ted's previous marriage. Barbara and Les Chambers lived at number 6 Maple Grove, they had Julie and Gary who will now be in their 50's. Barbara and Les are still with us in their early 80's and living in Halton-le-Clay.

The month was April still 1967 and I had heard Petrofina were wanting two drivers. Now back then this was a golden opportunity. So, I went down to the depot which was on the Humber Bank at North Killingholme, the interview was with a guy called John Young who was the General Manager of the depot. With the experience I had on previous tanker driving jobs in my favour, I was offered the job and couldn't wait to leave Caledonian and start work for Petrofina (known as Fina).

Back then you never got asked for a CV. All I had was the interview and a driving test in a small tanker with the Foreman of the service repair garage Fina had. Of course, that was quite easy as all it consisted of was to drive down the road, go up through the gear box and back down, then reverse into a road end and back to the depot.

I had applied to other petrol companies for driving jobs, and that very week I got the Fina job I was also offered a job at Gulf Oils, Texaco (which was Regent) Shell and BP, so I was spoilt for choice. Of course, I chose to stay with Fina and loved it.

My start date was early May 1967, and the delivery was to Tinsley Steel Sheffield (all long gone now) with fuel oil, a guy called Keith Phillips delivered a load of oil with me. Keith became a good friend at Fina and had a brother called Melvyn who also worked there. Melv became a life long friend.

Wash days at the bungalow were a challenge because we didnt have a washing machine in the early days, and with us both working we usually had to do the washing after tea on a Monday. Just for a few weeks until we got a washing machine, we would do the washing in the kitchen sink, rinsing them as best as we could and ringing them out in an old ringer which I had refurbished. I worked it while Marina fed the clothes through. We would have our wellingtons on whilst doing the whole washing procedure, and sometimes we even got a laugh!

It was about this time when Frank Watson came down one night after tea with a pair of kittens, a boy and girl. We decided to keep the girl and called her Smokey. The boy, Sam, as they called him went next door. As Smokey grew up she became affectionate and when I came home at night she would be there in the kitchen. I would scratch my shoulder to get her attention and she would look up at me with her big eyes and run up my overalls and sit on my shoulder. We enjoyed Smokey for fourteen years until we were forced to have her put to sleep.

About this time we got our first washing machine, it was an English Electric make (popular in its day) automatic and very heavy. I would wheel it across the kitchen floor to the sink so we could put the pipes on the taps. It was a heavy old sod with a front wheel jack that allowed you to move it. We had that for a few years before switching to a Twin Tub which Marina liked much better.

Whilst all this was going on I was still enjoying my driving job at Fina, and was also driving to Barton to have my hair cut with George because back then I was very particular and wouldn't let anyone near it except George.

The Summer went and Autumn was on the way. I had changed the Ford Anglia for another Ford but this one was a Zephyr 6. I sold the Anglia but can't remember to whom. I bought the Zephyr from a work mate called Arthur Woods, he was our union leader and a really good man but sadly not with us anymore. Glynn, our new neighbour and friend took me one Sunday morning to buy it.

Arthur lived at Barrow and wanted £20 for it so having looked around it I offered him £18 which he accepted. The year of the car was 1953 so that made it fourteen years old. In its day it was a luxury car and I was happy with my purchase. It was a column gear change with a bench seat and no seat belts. The seat belt law came into force in January 1983.

Like most Ford cars it was black with a six cylinder engine which was very hungry but back then all I can say is petrol wasn't a problem.

Shortly after the Zephyr, Glynn told me about a Standard 8 for sale, this was in Doncaster at Connie's Step-dad's house. The poor man had lost his eyesight and coudn't drive anymore. Glynn said it was for sale at £12 so I thought great, I could sell the Zephyr at a profit and buy the Standard which I did. The four of us travelled over to collect the car one Sunday morning, I paid for it and Connie travelled back with me whilst Glynn came back with Marina, driving the Zephyr. Now let me tell you about the Standard, it had a white roof with a dark green body and the speedometer would flicker on ten mile one way then the other way so you only got a rough idea of the speed you were travelling but it wouldn't go fast anyway, and it made a noise like a train on a track, "chuckatachak chuckatachak," and so on.

Our first Christmas was getting near but I can't remember much of what we did. I do remember enjoying my first darts league experience and my first win. It was so good winning for your team. Glynn and I had signed on for the Station Hotel Habrough and even back then Frank Watson, my mate, was playing for us as he still is today. A lot of the team, like Glynn, have died over the years and only five of us remain out of fourteen. However Frank and I are still enjoying playing for a team and will until we can't I guess.

The New Arrival

New Year 1968 arrived and the weather was very snowy. We found it a struggle to pay the mortgage as we were also paying endowment insurance alongside it, but we managed it because we were both working and I would do anything for extra cash.

With beautiful Spring on the way I was thinking of ways to earn more cash when one morning at work a guy called Stan Goodhand, knowing I had a coach licence known as a PSV, told me Mick Emmerson, a local coach operator wanted part-time drivers. Mick was a real nice guy and very hard working and was pleased to accept me as one of his drivers.

The work pattern at Fina was 4 x 10 hour days which gave you a lot of time off. For example if you started Monday then you completed your week on Thursday, and started again the following Wednesday, so this gave you five days off. Back then Mick had just bought the small coach company which was owned by local people called Sharp & Brumby. The coaches were an old Bedford, which we used mainly for school kids, the other one was also a Bedford and much newer and in its day was luxury. But it wasn't long before Mick added two more coaches, one was yet another Bedford but smaller, this was used for private parties and some school runs, the other one was a Thames Trader Coach which I enjoyed driving most.

One of my first private party jobs was taking out The Evergreens, who were a group of retired Immingham folk who formed the group for friendship and recreation and once a month would hire a coach from Mick to go on Mystery Tours, and trips to places like Mablethorpe, Skegness, and Cleethorpes. Also back in those days a few garden centres were beginning to open with tea shops and we would take the Evergreens there too.

I soon got to know them all very well and formed a good relationship with them. There were one or two of them that found the coach steps hard work so I would help them on and off which they loved and after a while they would ask Mick if I was available to drive them. Of course the other part-time drivers would call me the favourite but that didn't bother me because my helping hand reflected in the tips at the end of the day out.

I will stay with my coaching days and tell you about the mystery trips I did for Mr and Mrs Clarke. They lived in Sherwood Avenue, Grimsby and had a wonderful group of people in thier sixties, and all members of "The Trip Club" as they called it. My first trip for them was round the wold villages finishing up at The Salutation Inn near Caistor.

It was on this trip that I met Mrs Cooke, what a character! I soon got to know her sense of humour. When everyone was on the coach and someone said, "Where are we going driver?" Mrs Cooke said; "Mervin doesen't know our destination and to make it special I have to blindfold him so nobody knows where we are heading! Ha ha."

More trips followed with the Clarke's Gang and we always had a good laugh. After the pub visits they all wanted a sing song; same old songs all from the war days and there were some good singers too.

Mick said one morning after we got back in off the school runs, "How do you fancy the weekend at Blackpool with the Clarke's Gang? They have asked for you to take them to see the illuminations."

Now these runs were good money so I jumped at the chance and all it required was for me to change my days off at Fina.

The coach for the weekend was a two year old Bedford and remember the single decker coaches of that era could only carry forty one passengers. Picking them all up on that special morning was quite exciting, seeing them all smiling and chatting about the journey over the Pennines.

We had a tea and a 'wee' stop at Doncaster, (that's what the ladies called it) and in those days the stop was in the market square where there were two lovely little tea shops to accommodate us all. Being the driver, I used to get my food and drink for free. Sadly the old market and cafes have long gone to make way for an ugly multistory car park and offices.

The journey with a stop could take four and a half hours at least, so on arriving at Blackpool our passengers were ready for a leg stretch and another cuppa. Our humble hotel was in Parliament Street which had many more B&B's and hotels close by.

I can't remember what we did for the rest of the day but let me tell you about going to bed! I had just got settled down and was feeling sleepy when there was a tap on my bedroom door. I said, "Hello who is it?" When I heard who it was, (Mrs Cooke!) I thought "Oh no!"

She said, "We've come for our good night kiss Mervin."

When I opened the door there were four of them laughing and giggling. I can't remember how I got around it but I did and wished them good night. Then came the morning and they all sat down for breakfast chatting away and smiling at me saying, "Good morning Mervin, did you sleep well?"

"Yes," I said, "How are you all?"

"Oh we're fine Mervin," said Mrs Cooke, smiling.

I got sat down and tipped some cornflakes in to my dish, I noticed the milk was on the next table so as I turned around to ask for it, as quick as a flash Mrs Cooke had put two black plastic spiders in my cornflakes, well hidden I may say. So as I started eating, one popped up! What a shock! Of course the breakfast room was in uproar, and Mrs Cooke laughed her head off along with alot more. I saw the funny side and had a joke about it, but it never went away and I wasn't allowed to forget that one. There was a lot more like that with Mrs Cooke and the gang but I loved it.

Going around the lights at Blackpool was a slow old job, stop, start every few yards and by the time you got around and out the other end, you were faced with the long drive home over the Pennines and all of the towns, arriving in the early hours of Sunday morning, then parking the coach after having mopped out the floor for the following driver. And I did that trip quite a few times.

But Mrs Cooke, Mr and Mrs Clarke and the gang always had a good whip round for me. It was common for me to get £5 as well as being payed by Mick but I can't remember exactly what he paid.

On darts match nights if the team were playing away I would collect the small coach and pick the lads up, then off we would go to the Barton area and sometimes as far out as West Halton near Scunthorpe. I drove the coaches part time until our work pattern changed at Fina, this would be late 1969. I enjoyed driving them and have some good memories.

Bill Laite was one of Mick's full-time drivers and a bit rough and ready but a really good bloke. I remember one morning we had all got back off the school runs and as usual we would stand in the office having a chat about coaching runs, that day Bill decided to tell us about his 'tummy upset', just let me tell you Mick was quite a gentleman and didn't swear much or talk about unsavoury things. So Bill talked about his tummy upset in fine detail.

Mick's face was a picture of disgust and he said;

"Bill do we have to know about your body funtions like this?"

Bill said; "Well I was only tellin ya how me arse was sore an all!"

So that was Bill, salt of the earth but a rough diamond. Sadly both Mick and Bill have passed on now. The coach company was run by his widow Marion for a while then sold out to a chap called Alan Brumby, who sold out to a larger company in 2010. The old depot down Bluestone Lane has gone now, just derelict land, but memories of my coaching days are still with me and the memory of Bill of course.

Whilst my coaching days were going on I was also enjoying my Fina job on the tankers. Fina had a depot in Peterborough and in the summer months when their drivers were on holiday one or two of our drivers had to go down to Peterborough to cover for them.

Summer 1968 was my turn to go for one week. Remember early in the year I had bought an old Standard 8 car with a white roof, dark green body, well Marina and I thought it would be nice to have it in a cream colour. We didn't have much to do at Peterborough so I began to undercoat the old car a yellow colour. I had got the front part done when John the Manager came out of the office with some deliveries for me.

He said "Sorry Merv but we have these few to do now."

So there I am with a three-tone colour car and I didn't have time to do any more that week as I was kept busy on deliveries. So Friday came and it was time to go home and I remember it was about the first week in July and I hadn't taxed the car. Back in those days with no national computer at Swansea to track vehicles you had fourteen days grace at the beginning of the month to do it.

I left the Peterborough depot about 2pm, heading home, and I hadn't spoken to Marina all week because we hadn't a phone. I remember going through Lincoln in my little three-tone colour car not taxed and thinking nothing of it. I'm thinking you couldn't do that today!

I couldn't wait to get back home again to Marina and Smokey, our little cat.

Back then we were friendly with Malc Hardy and his then wife Bobbie, and after a night out, we had decided to all go on holiday to Cornwall. Malc had a nice car, it was a Ford Cortina Estate, so having booked our holidays from work we arranged to go early September. We didn't book any B&B, we just packed a case, and I remember we went over to Malc and Bobbie's, left our car at their place and off we went.

That's what you did in those days, there was no need to book anywhere. For one thing, there weren't as many people in the country or traffic on the roads.

Recalling this memory makes me think how lucky we were to have lived through those wonderful care free days.

The holiday was lovely with a good B&B and hot weather. I can't remember how much we paid for digs or how much money we took with us but we had a good time. I do remember the man who ran the B&B was a retired dentist and his wife, who had a whistle when she spoke! Malc and I thought he had made her false teeth a bit dodgy so he got a giggle every time she spoke. We had a good laugh at her at breakfast listening to her ask us what we would like with that wonderful lisp.

After our holiday we were back home busy working and getting our home ship shape, when after we had finished our tea one night Marina looked at me a little strange and said; "I think I'm pregnant!"

I said "Wow that's fantastic!" and gave her a big hug but unfortunately she didn't think so. Anyway after a visit to the doctors it was confirmed we were expecting our first child, 'Kerry,' and after a few weeks Marina was as excited as I was.

Her first reaction was a little negative because she didn't think we were ready, but as I explained you're never ready, you just have to welcome it with open arms and do your best!

Of course in those days you didn't know what you were going to get. No ultrasounds then to let you know.

I remember she was very sick in the mornings for a few weeks but that eventually went away.

The end of the summer arrived and I still hadn't painted the old Standard, so that would be be my next project. I got it totally undercoated one Saturday, then on the Sunday glossed it up a lovely pale cream. The colour was called 'Silver Gleam,' and I have to say it looked well.

The Standard did us a good service, because I had painted it with Dulux house paint and it would get black dirt streaks down the side after it rained and eventually wouldn't come off. So like most people would wash their car on a Sunday morning, I would go out and paint mine, making it look like new again. Now I didn't think that was funny at the time, but recalling the memory now it sounds so silly. But that's the stuff I used to do.

Back then we had log books to detail our journey regarding breaks etc. and Fina gave us eight hours for the Nottingham run, giving us plenty of free time (for darts), so every other week through Winter 1968/69 I played for The Traveller's Rest, and it was a bit of a joke around Fina like, "Dove'y is playing darts for a pub at Newark!"

Talking about it now I can't believe I did it. Even the shift supervisor would ask; "How did the darts go tonight Merv?"

Then of course the other weeks when I was on mornings I played for The Station at Habrough. Ah, good days and lovely memories.

Christmas came and went and by then I was busy getting the small bedroom ready for our new arrival, while Marina was busy knitting little coats and everything that new babies require. She was very good at knitting and sewing, making all kinds of things. I remember in the early Spring we went to Pramland at Cleethorpes to choose our new pram. Marina chose a Marmet cream and navy pram, this was top of the range in its day.

We used to visit Gran and Pop on a regular basis and I can remember Gran was always so pleased to see us and would say to Pop how pleased my Mam would have been had she been alive.

It's so sad now writing about this because at the time we were young and full of excitement with our new baby on the way and I don't think we fully understood how poor Gran and Pop felt. They had experienced losing a daughter and we hadn't. But I believe loved ones who have passed on are still with us in spirit and can see all that they want to see.

This belief I have gives me a warm feeling that they're near, and that goodbye isn't that final, just a temporary cheerio and I will see you later.

We were also visiting Pearl and John who at that time lived in Althorpe near Scunthorpe. Pearl was quite excited about the birth date we had been given because it was close to her birthday.

The day finally came in May when it was time to take Marina into the maternity home. She had been having pains on a regular basis so the midwife advised us it was time. So we piled into the old Standard with everything that was required for the new baby and Mum's stay. I wasn't allowed to stay with her and had to come home.

Back then we weren't on the phone, so we had given them Connie's telephone number, who lived across the road from us. I will never forget that same afternoon on May 20th 1969, it was about tea-time and I had decided to cut the front lawn. I had just about done it, when Connie called across and said, "Hey up Merv you're a dad! Marina has just given birth to a beautiful baby girl."

I couldn't believe it. My first baby girl.

I always think how lucky we were to have two healthy girls who have grown up now to make us feel so proud of what they have given us back with their love, care, and achievements in their life.

But that's another story, to carry on in another book.

MERVIN DOVE

Mervin Dove was born in 1941 in North Lincolnshire and spent a varied and playful childhood in Barton upon Humber.

Mervin has had a distinctive and diverse career which involved everything from tractor driving, to chimney sweeping, to tanker driving. Inspired by his artistic background, he completed a two-year college course in signwriting and went on to build his reputation part time.

In September 1983, Mervin left Petrofina to pursue his hobby full time. He has never looked back.

Now with a successful client base and reputable company, Mervin is one of the few traditional signwriters in the area keeping the profession alive in its traditional form. His work includes signwriting vintage lorries, boats, trucks, shops, chalk board art and menus, ice cream vans and much more.

Mervin originally decided to write his story as a keepsake for his children. But after gaining an incredible response from the public, Mervin has now taken the decision to share his story with the world. He is a natural storyteller and is currently working on his second book.